HOPE *when it's* HEAVY

TRUSTING GOD IS GOOD WHEN YOUR SEASON IS NOT

This book belongs on every believer's bookshelf. Every life has seasons during which it's difficult to see the goodness of God. This book is an honest look at those seasons, packed with biblical insights and practical applications that will make it personal to every reader. With warmth and wisdom, Amy offers a steadying hand, a balm to the soul, and most importantly, hope—even when it's heavy.

—Jocelyn Green, coauthor of *Faith Deployed: Daily Encouragement for Military Wives* and *The 5 Love Languages Military Edition*

Amy introduces a hopeful and theological approach to the mystery of suffering in this book. With humble authenticity, she courageously pens words of wisdom birthed from her own seasons of heartbreak and disappointment. This book will challenge and guide its readers to faithfully steward adversity to the glory of God.

—Sheneka Land, MDiv, ordained minister and clinical chaplain

This is a must-read for any woman carrying the weight of an uncertain future. Amy's words are a powerful reminder that even in the hardest moments, hope is never out of reach. Amy's words will meet you where you are and gently point you toward a future filled with grace, courage, and unwavering love. This book is not just about enduring hard seasons, it's about finding purpose and hope in them. And for every woman who feels like her story is too broken, too messy, or too uncertain, this book is proof that God is still writing something beautiful.

—Annie Tang Humphrey, Chief Operating Officer at Save the Storks

Amy's words challenge me to cultivate an "even though . . . I will" faith in God, the kind of faith that endures even in life's heaviest moments. Whether grappling with loss, broken relationships, financial hardship, or the deep wounds of grief and church hurt, readers will find both solace and strength in these pages. With hard-won wisdom and profound practicality, Amy speaks directly to the heart of every woman navigating deep struggles. This book is a wellspring of hope, offering reassurance in the midst of pain and the courage to persevere.

—Brenda Pace, DMin, speaker and author of *Journey of a Military Wife*

In the midst of life's hardest seasons, Amy does not offer empty platitudes but a compassionate hand to hold. With vulnerability and deep biblical wisdom, she invites us to wrestle with our questions and burdens, always pointing us back to the unwavering hope we have in Christ. This book is both a lifeline and a light in the darkness—one that will meet readers in their pain and walk with them toward healing and trust.

—Rachael Adams, author of *A Little Goes a Long Way* and *Everyday Prayers for Love*

This book is a heartfelt reflection on having faith in hard seasons. With honesty and care, Amy shares her own struggles while reminding readers that God welcomes our doubts and questions. Her writing feels like a conversation with a trusted friend—real, thoughtful, and encouraging. I appreciate Amy's ability to recognize pain without rushing past it, while pointing to the steady hope we have in Christ, who works through both joy and pain. This is a great reminder that even when life is overwhelming, we're never alone.

—**Cara Hicks**, Founder and Chief Empowerment Officer at The MOMentum Network

This book is an amazing gift for anyone needing to find or fight for hope in a hard season. Amy's poignant writing is a kind invitation to the weary soul who wants to feel they are not alone during their hard season. Amy does a beautiful job of drawing the reader to find hope in the Lord while also granting the reader the grace to wrestle. As a trained counselor, I would recommend this book as a helpful resource for clients who are struggling through difficult times. It will be a gift to those in need of hope. Amy's writing style is like having coffee with a trusted friend, so as a reader, you will find safety in this journey.

—**Jennifer Hand**, author of *My Yes is on the Table*, Executive Director of Coming Alive Ministries

Amy is real, her story is real. This book gives real tangible insights into scripture and her own heart as to how to navigate your own heavy, hoping soul. Her writing comes from a place of heart and experiential knowledge not just head knowledge. She "knows" the Savior who she hopes in. This is an invitation into that knowing, and into hope even when your heart is heavy with grief, health, loss or whatever circumstance life has brought to your door.

—**Sandy Hallcox**, Founder and President of Acts244 Ministry

Through the hard seasons, we desperately need the kind of hope, anchored and sure, that doesn't ignore the weight and the wrestle that Amy offers in this book. Whether you're walking through the hard, or love someone who is, her unique combination of qualifications and experiences along with her deep love for Jesus enable Amy to guide our path to healing for our whole person (physically, emotionally and spiritually) with nuance and such grace. This book is gentle enough to read in the midst of hardship or relatable enough we can read it to supply tools and frameworks for the next time we face the wrestle.

—**Meleah Smith**, Communications Consultant

HOPE when it's HEAVY

TRUSTING GOD IS GOOD WHEN YOUR SEASON IS NOT

AMY EATON

Hope When It's Heavy
Trusting God is Good When Your Season is Not

Copyright © 2025 by Amy Eaton

All rights reserved. No part of this publication may be reproduced, stored in a retrieval system, or transmitted in any form or by any means - electronic, mechanical, photocopy, recording, scanning or any other - except for brief quotations in printed reviews or articles, without the prior permission of the author.

Unless otherwise noted, all Scripture quotations are taken from the ESV® Bible (The Holy Bible, English Standard Version®), copyright © 2001 by Crossway, a publishing ministry of Good News Publishers. Used by permission. All rights reserved.

Scripture quotations marked (NIV) are taken from the Holy Bible, New International Version®, NIV®. Copyright © 1973, 1978, 1984, 2011 by Biblica, Inc.™ Used by permission of Zondervan. All rights reserved worldwide. www.zondervan.comThe "NIV" and "New International Version" are trademarks registered in the United States Patent and Trademark Office by Biblica, Inc.™

Scripture quotations marked (NLT) are taken from the Holy Bible, New Living Translation, copyright ©1996, 2004, 2015 by Tyndale House Foundation. Used by permission of Tyndale House Publishers, Carol Stream, Illinois 60188. All rights reserved.

Scripture quotations marked MSG are taken from The Message, copyright © 1993, 2002, 2018 by Eugene H. Peterson. Used by permission of NavPress. All rights reserved. Represented by Tyndale House Publishers.

Scripture quotations marked TPT are from The Passion Translation®. Copyright © 2017, 2018, 2020 by Passion & Fire Ministries, Inc. Used by permission. All rights reserved. ThePassionTranslation.com.

Scripture quotations marked (AMPC) taken from the Amplified® Bible, Copyright © 1954, 1958, 1962, 1964, 1965, 1987 by The Lockman Foundation. Used by permission. lockman.org

ISBN: 978-1-7363419-1-9
eBook ISBN: 978-1-7363419-3-3

Cover and interior design by Sharon VanLoozenoord and Dustin Hysinger
Editing by Nycole Sinks
Cover art from an oil painting titled "Going Home,"
   a gift to the author by her aunt, Ann Brown Thomason.
   Used by permission. AnnBrownThomason.com
Author photo by Zach Camp, zachcamp.com

Printed in the United States of America
First edition

To the one who feels like she's holding on by a thread,

you are so deeply loved.

Jesus alone brings hope, light, and peace.

This book is dedicated to you,

and I hope you'll find encouragement

and reminders of His kindness within these pages.

Contents

INTRODUCTION
Why I hope you will read this book
1

CHAPTER 1
Even though I feel overwhelmed
7

CHAPTER 2
Even though the world feels scary
23

CHAPTER 3
Even though I feel alone
39

CHAPTER 4
Even though there are no answers
53

CHAPTER 5
Even though I am hurting
67

CHAPTER 6
I will choose to . . .
83

ACKNOWLEDGMENTS
97

ENDNOTES
99

Introduction
Why I Hope You Will Read This Book

"Is this Mrs. Eaton?" The caller's tone was cold and focused. This was not good news. As he spoke, I spiraled so swiftly that I had to lean against a nearby wall, very grateful for the miracle that no one else was in the large conference room. Just a half hour earlier, I had wrapped up a successful leadership project and was floating on cloud nine. In a matter of seconds, my world shifted as I received devastating news, and I left work immediately.

Driving home I could not contain my sobbing. I was incredibly angry. Angry at this situation, angry at the caller, angry that this was happening today or even at all. And I was so very angry at God. I pray often. I have Exodus 14:14 on the wall of my living room, an art piece that has followed me through multiple houses as a reminder that God fights on our behalf. But clearly, He was nowhere to be found in *this*. As I drove, I prayed and processed with Him. I shouted so desperately and angrily that my voice pitched and broke, "FIGHT FOR ME! YOU PROMISED YOU WOULD FIGHT FOR ME!"

I've experienced many hard things in my lifetime, most of which occurred after I became a Christian. It perplexes me when people assume that Christianity is meant to be only joy and sunshine, prosperity and rainbows. Such a belief is clearly not reality. I have never met a Christ-follower who has had a pain-free, trial-free story. I've honestly never met a human without a trail of difficulty they've had to trudge through.

But as a Christian, I wrestle with this weird, self-imposed necessity to have a positive answer for the tough questions of life, as though God's reputation and promises are resting upon my inadequate shoulders and words. Yet many questions don't have answers neatly tied with a bow. Many are a tangled mess with seemingly no explanation or method for untangling.

And here are you and I, in the middle of pain and difficulty, attempting to wrestle with our confusions and doubts among the messiness. But what if we all put down our "I'm fine" masks and chose to be vulnerable? What if we were brave enough to sit in the unknown, while closely wrapped in the loving arms of our Father? Is it possible we could bring to Him all of our thoughts, emotions, joys, and difficulties? What if we took our anger and confusion to Him?

Habakkuk, King David, Job, and others in the Bible have done this very thing, and we have their messy wonderings timelessly captured within the pages of God's Holy Word. If those wrestlings and challenging dialogues with God are important enough that He included them in the Bible, then they're an important reminder for us to wrestle out our own wonderings with Him, too.

I am thankful to know God on a deep enough level that I'm aware of this truth: God is the safest place to take my anger and brokenness. I don't know about you, but I don't want a social-media-worthy picture of God. I want a redeemer! A warrior, a mighty tower with infinite strength, not just a "friend" to post feed-worthy images of. I want Him to pull me close and not be someone who would turn me away when I throw something, sob, or crumble. I want a God who will meet me *here*—again. A God who gives me second, fifth, and seventy-times-seven chances. Perhaps you want to know this God, too?

During a particularly hard time, trying to process all the heavy things happening in my world, I wrote this to the Lord in my journal:

> *Do you weep?*
> *Do you weep when a child has fallen?*
> *When a storm ravages a town?*
> *Do you shed tears or hurt with us,*
> *when everything seems to go wrong?*
> *Does your heart ache like a mother,*
> *when her child takes his own life?*
> *Do you kneel down with us?*

> *Do you cry by our side?*
> *God, sometimes I want to picture you as one who comes close, holds us, and mourns with us (Psalm 34:18). And sometimes I want to picture you as the strong tower of infinite strength I know you to be (Psalm 73:28).*
> *And really, I want both.*
> *Both, and.*
> *I'm so grateful you are beyond my human comprehension.*
> *I don't desire or trust in what man can do.*
> *"When the earth and all its people quake,*
> *it is I who hold its pillars firm." (Psalm 75:3 NIV)*

Habakkuk, an Old Testament prophet, proclaimed this to God as he looked out upon the mess of his world:

> How long, O LORD, must I call for help?
> But you do not listen!
> "Violence is everywhere!" I cry,
> but you do not come to save.
> Must I forever see these evil deeds?
> Why must I watch all this misery?
> Wherever I look,
> I see destruction and violence.
> I am surrounded by people
> who love to argue and fight.
> (Habakkuk 1:2-3 NLT)

This is clearly a cry of desperation, as Habakkuk bravely calls upon the only One in whom peace and victory reside. I know this cry. I have also cried out in desperation, presenting my hard questions to this God I know personally, though sometimes I feel so far from Him when I look at the messy world around me.

I may not know you personally, but one thing I'm certain of—you have walked through some hard and heavy things. No individual or generation is spared, and Habakkuk's cries remind me that we've been wrestling with brokenness in this world since sin entered the equation. None of us are exempt from experiencing or facing difficulties.

I am personally in the middle of another difficult season right now. As a military mom, I miss out on so much with my son and his beautiful growing family. Though I've savored every second, I've only been able to visit with him on four occasions in the last five years as he is stationed overseas. I've had minimal time with him, my precious daughter in love, and my granddaughter due to the miles and lives that separate us. Though difficult, it's only one hard thing I'm wrestling with in this season, some of which I cannot and won't speak to in such a public space as a published book.

I lost my father to a terribly swift and arduous battle with unexpected cancer. I saw the greed of others in ways that broke my heart as I navigated honoring his wishes with his belongings after his death.

I have dearly loved family members I must choose healthy boundaries with, though it aches my heart as I long for a different reality with them. One where we can have a relationship and be healthily present in each other's lives.

We have friends we've lost too soon, navigated parental loss alongside close friends, lost pets whom we deeply loved, and so much more. It's not just the big hard things like loss, the little things that feel like a leaking, never-ending faucet can be hard and heavy, too.

My job is significantly demanding, requiring long hours that I am not sure I have the capacity to give at times. When writing the first half of this book, my husband was still in the military and away on active duty. He has been away many times over the years of our marriage due to military service, which has often left me wrestling with much of the grief and processing of life's difficulties without him near.

In the hardest seasons, if it weren't for the Lord, I have feared I would break, and yet, my story is so small compared to the story of grief and difficulty others are facing.

I also have several close friends currently walking out a difficult Job-like story, as I love and hold them in prayer. I'm deeply grateful

God doesn't leave us abandoned to be consumed with our grief or fear. He Himself is our peace, and He has created us with tools to help battle these difficulties. Better still, He has given us clarity in His Holy Word. I sometimes wonder what I have to add when He's given us what we need in the Bible, but I cannot shake the call on my heart to keep showing up to write these words as He leads.

Habakkuk inspires me in his ability to follow up his honest wrestlings and those "even though" statements in verse 17 with declaring "yet I will rejoice in the Lord; I will take joy in the God of my salvation" (Habakkuk 3:18). I hope as you navigate the pages of this book, you'll find you are not alone in your wonderings or wrestlings. And that God is the very best place to bring your honesty. May you wrap up your reading with a deeper understanding of the goodness of God, regardless of circumstance, and the tools and gifts He's given you to navigate the hard and heavy seasons of this life in His strength. And then, you too can say, "even though . . . I will."

Chapter One
Even though I feel overwhelmed

"Did God really say you must not eat the fruit
from any of the trees in the garden?"—Satan

"Of course we may eat fruit from the trees in the garden. . . .
It's only the fruit from the tree in the middle
of the garden that we are not allowed to eat. God said,
'You must not eat it or even touch it;
if you do, you will die.'"—Eve

"You won't die. . . . God knows that your eyes will be opened
as soon as you eat it, and you will be like God,
knowing both good and evil."—Satan
(Excerpts from Genesis 3:1–5 NLT)

Why Is It So Easy to Bite the Apple?

I'm a huge fan of therapy and have personally benefited from it at various points in my life. One such time though, the Lord had been encouraging me to start a therapy journey for around a year before I gave an obedient yes. I pondered a thousand reasons why I didn't need to go, so I kept putting it off: I'm emotionally healthy, I have strong coping skills and grit. I'm happy, and those scales I fill out at a doctor's office or my annual screening for the wellness program at work suggest I'm fine.

But, as I listened to this nudge from the Lord, I realized I was somewhere between being grateful for every good thing in my life and becoming aware of some heart wounds that needed mending. My heart wounds seemed to be the most evident when I was navigating difficult seasons.

I was also beginning to realize the importance of the question "why?" When I noticed an uncharacteristic response within myself, I learned to ask: why did I think or respond in that way? Where might that be coming from, is there a wound with a root I've not tended to? I'm no green thumb or gardening expert, but I know that roots are a vital part of a plant. When looking at a plant we only see above the surface, we don't see a plant's roots. That inability to see the deep, hidden parts does not change their importance or impact. Roots are a vital part of what fuels the plant, but they also hold it firm within the ground when storms, floods, and hardships come.

In the context of our identity, roots are important and vital, too. We are shaped and influenced by our experiences in ways we may never fully understand, though trained therapists can help us dig deep into discovery and possible healing. Partnership with a trained expert was a key I was missing.

I had been on a journey of pursuing spiritual and emotional healing and maturity. It now became clear, I was to begin a new personal therapy journey as I walked through the spiritual development I was already navigating.

I don't know about you, but I do not want to carry generational unhealthiness any further into my lineage. Every family has some, and I want my generational unhealth to stop here. I want to be the change in my family that shifts our future for eternity—for God's glory. In order to do this though, I have to be willing to open up and let the healing light of God in to reveal what is in need of healing.

Like a splinter ignored, even something small can fester and become significant or create a negative impact. I am no longer satisfied with excusing or ignoring, and I am not even OK with blaming my roots. I want to know what might need tended within the garden of my heart and welcome the love of Christ to wash over and heal every part of me.

One gift received in my healing journey is self-awareness. I am keenly aware that I am captured by the pull of people-pleasing. This is certainly one of the areas in my heart the Lord wants me to root out and heal. At the start of the journey, my therapist gently pointed out that I'm not in crisis, and I have no major mental health issues. So, she asked thoughtfully . . . why was I there? What was my goal for therapy? Her curiosity spoke a spirit-led and discerning *"You're here for a reason, Amy; let's prayerfully choose a goal and focus where He's leading you"* invitation.

Strange as it may seem, I honestly did not know why I started therapy that day. All I knew was God was calling me out into this ocean of a healing journey that felt bigger than me, and He was telling me that therapy was going to be an important part of it all, even though I felt "OK." As the time passed until my next session, I prayed often. The Lord revealed a significant heart-weed; it was an identity-influencing lie that I believed of myself. A lie with roots so deep they were not going to easily give way to removal. That people-pleasing nature? The roots are so deep, it's as though they're wrapped up in my bones.

One of the most prominent lies that I fight with is that I am not enough. Upon being able to name it, the Lord helped me to prayerfully chase down that lie to discern what thoughts might be reinforcing it. This was accomplished by considering what that statement means to me and what I'm afraid of if that statement is true. I invited the Holy Spirit to help me see, and through prayer and sitting with my heart and mind, the thoughts were exposed in this order: if I'm not enough, I'm not liked. If I'm not liked, I'm not loved. If I'm not loved, I'm not needed—and if I'm not needed, *then I will be abandoned.* Insert all the teary, sobbing emojis here—I don't love admitting that private thought trail so publicly, but I've seen where this transparency has encouraged other women in my close circle to consider their own thought trails, too. Perhaps you have experienced a similar thought trail? If so, you are not alone.

These hidden thoughts were lies that branched off the first one, fortifying the entangled root system. I discovered the root of the first lie by chasing down the connected hidden thoughts. This helped me to see just how deeply rooted the driver behind my people-pleasing tendencies had become.

These are lies I still wrestle with today. Unless I'm paying attention and looking for their presence, I'll fall victim to entertaining them without even thinking of it. I have to actively and consciously remind myself that my identity is fully secured within Christ. Not earned by anything I do or anyone's affection I may receive. I must be intentional with my heart-thoughts and not allow them to wander wherever they may wish to roam.

An important example of being attentive to my heart-thoughts can be seen in my relationship with my husband. He is naturally wired for efficiency and leadership, and all his personality assessments agree. He served in the military for over twenty years and has a straightforward nature when delivering information. He has a gift for seeing more efficient ways of doing things and loves to share that wisdom. It's genuinely a beautiful thing, and many have benefited from his giftings, me included. However, if the foundation for my worth and value lie in the way his words and tone make me feel from one moment to the next, I am setting both of us up for frequent failure.

Another unique opportunity the Lord brought into my life is a two-year small group journey focused on caring for my soul. As I journeyed through the chapters and vulnerable sharing with my friends, I learned that I wrestle deeply with identity. In my conversations and research, I'm learning how very common that identity battle is—we are not alone. Can I just say that I've been comforted by realizing that so many others wrestle with this, too? There's something about not feeling alone in your wrestlings.

How kind is God that He would reveal these spaces in need of healing to me! I pray He does the same for you if there are any spaces in your heart in need of His grace, love, and light. He is gentle, patient, and kind in His delivery. I'd love to share a recent example of His healing work in my heart.

Not long ago, my husband and I walked alongside our friends as they were saying goodbye to their mom who was like a mom to us, too. I would call her "Other Mama" sometimes because she was like another mom to us; my husband had been best friends with one of her sons since they were ten. I even met her before I met any of his family! Other Mama's name was Teresea.

Her final weeks were heartbreaking, yet her love for Jesus and the peace of God that was with her was evident and comforting. I was blessed with the opportunity to visit and sing to her during her hospice days. There I sat by her bedside asking her what song she'd like me to sing next. Her absolute favorite hymn is "How Great Thou Art," and she loved the Carrie Underwood version (no pressure!).

I was a worship leader for over ten years at the church Teresea attended, and during those years I often wrestled with lies of not-enoughness. Every time I stepped out onto that stage, I was both keenly aware of how unworthy I was (even as I strived to live a holy life) and terrified of how not-enough I was in the shadow of the incredibly gifted and trained vocalists I shared that space with.

Teresea loved my voice and loved to see me sing because I was like another daughter to her. Singing by her side in those sacred moments was so special, but I admit I had specifically avoided singing "How Great Thou Art" for years because it's a difficult hymn to sing. And as an untrained vocalist, it was my Achilles' heel when it came to traditional hymns.

I knew I'd be asked to sing it at her services, and I truly wanted to, but I was also so afraid of failure. I loved her enough though that I was willing to put in the work to be ready to sing it at her services, so I began practicing immediately when her son approached me and asked me to sing.

I often failed at the most difficult switch within the song and was getting so angry, and I cried out to God to help me during my solo practice sessions. I would continue practicing and then jump over to the next thing on my to-do list, never pausing to let Him help me where I truly needed His help: in my heart. The Lord used my therapist and small group to show me what was happening in my heart in those moments.

The reality was that I was still wrestling with that decades-old lie that I could never be enough because I didn't meet some standard I had created in my mind of what others wanted me to be. On the day of Teresea's funeral, I was driving to my pre-scheduled therapy appointment (Coincidence? Definitely not!), and I, once again, was mad as I missed the part. In that moment, God spoke to me by bringing the chorus to my mind for the song "Jireh" by Elevation Worship & Maverick City Music. So, I put the song on repeat and turned up the volume high as I worshipped through my tears. I was reminded that Teresea had told me, "I will hear you" during the last time I sang over her and talked with her on this side of heaven. While I sang, I was reminded of one of my last conversations with Teresea. Someone mentioned me singing at her funeral and she told me, "I will hear you."

Here I was, still wrestling with my performance-driven lies; I knew that I wanted this to be perfect so that it could be a beautiful memory for everyone to hold dear, not a distraction. The Lord had my attention this time, though, and He silenced the lies when He reiterated: I am already loved and chosen by her, by her family, and most importantly—by God Himself. They loved me, not because of what I could do for them or how well I could perform. They simply loved *me*. They wanted my heart and voice because it mattered to their mom (and to them).

All God wanted me to do was to be free, to stand on the truth and foundation of HIS infinite and unconditional love for me. And that was enough. He was asking me, *"Amy, am I enough?"* And my heart shouted a resounding "Yes!" through my tears! (PS—The song went perfectly, and I was SO incredibly free as I sang over her that one last time. And out of that freedom, it was one of the most controlled vocal moments of all my years of singing. To Christ alone be all glory.)

There's interesting science that explains what I was experiencing, and I want to explore it with you here because it is truly empowering to realize the way God has intentionally made our bodies. When I was working on the master's thesis for my MS in psychology, I focused heavily on learning about and understanding the exploration and application of a theory researchers called self-determination theory. In essence, this theory claims that we adults have three core needs: autonomy, competence, and relatedness.

Here's how I like to explain these three pieces. Autonomy is our need for a level of control in the world around us and assurance that our decisions lead to outcomes we influenced or guided them to. Competence is saying that we have knowledge and it enables us to be successful in our world. Relatedness is our relational drive and nature; we all want to mean something to others and be in relationship with them.

All of this matters to you and me because if self-determination theory is true, then these are core motivating needs. And if these are our core motivating needs, then when those needs are threatened, we want to go on the defensive and self-protect.

The Bible is clear: we live in a world with good and evil, and we absolutely have an enemy and he wants to destroy us not just for the damnation of our souls but also seeks to destroy, distract, and waste our lived lives. One of his most effective tools is to get us to believe his lies. I've come to notice that the enemy's lies seem to always be half-truths, just enough truth to get me to listen but enough lie to get me off track.

Think about it. If the devil told you the sky was eggplant purple, and you have strong eyes and color sight, you know it's a lie. But if he says "Your husband didn't say thank you at dinner . . . He never says thank you . . . In fact, he made an interesting expression when eating and hardly looked up from his phone . . . Your dinner was awful, you can't keep the house organized, the children are a disaster, and you are to blame . . . I bet he doesn't really love you anymore." Yikes!

He hooked you with the half-truth: your husband didn't say the words "thank you" at dinner. Then, he took you down a road that caused you to state your fears and doubts with other half-truths and the spiral can happen that quick!

Let's unpack a different possibility. Sure, your husband might've been distracted by his phone, but you didn't ask what was so intriguing nor have you agreed on a no phones at the table rule yet. The house might be in disarray, but (insert natural explanation for your crazy busy week here), and it isn't always this way, or perhaps you need more help in this season of life. He did make a face when eating, but it could've been that the article he was reading had him upset, or you forgot he doesn't love chunks of onions in his chili. Your kids may very well be little terrors this week, but so are everyone's kids at this age, and with all they've had going on lately in their own worlds—of course they're going to act out.

There are a number of stories we could create here with the minimum facts we have, and if we focus on our feelings, they'll infer meaning that we cannot state factually as absolutely certain and true. It seems the enemy knows how to jump on the feelings train and take us straight to a place that can cut us deep or cause us to believe things that are not true.

What Satan is doing here is identifying something that is untrue and twisting it into something that feels probable but gets your eyes off Truth (capital "T" truth—the person of truth—Jesus Himself, and the Holy Word of God, the Bible). Thereby, he is causing you to question your core needs, making your foundation feel shaky and at risk of crumbling. If he can get you to doubt Truth, he can get you to think your foundation is faulty. And if you don't trust the foundation of God in your life, you'll revert to a need for control. This will manifest itself in different ways depending on how you respond to stress or the loss of control.

Perhaps you will blow up and storm out. Perhaps you will self-medicate with too much wine, food, activity, or another substance. Maybe you will pretend everything is fine while seething anger or bitterness grips your heart like a strangling vine, choking out the true love and compassion you have for your husband. Or perhaps you will dominate the moment, bulldozing over the hearts of your husband or children (or other loved ones in your life) and blame them for the carnage.

Friend, I'm not trying to paint a harsh picture of you—I've been guilty of thinking unfairly and reacting in ways I'm not proud of—I'm simply telling you that on the other side of such pain, there's wonderful joy ahead if you'll let the light of Truth in. There's freedom found when you stand on the foundation of God's love and His truth! You can be free of this easy-target mentality and learn to recognize these lies the instant they happen, take them captive (2 Corinthians 10:5), and renew your mind to refocus upon Truth (Romans 12:2)!

God created us in such a way that this is all scientifically possible! The enemy knows how our brains were made, too, and that's why he loves this tactic. But we can take heart because we know we are more than conquerors, and we have the tools we need to fight! Let's explore some facts about the brain and understand more about why we so easily follow these lie thought patterns that can overwhelm us.

Well-Worn Paths Are Great Lie-Foundations

We started this chapter with a question: why is it so easy to bite the apple? Eve and Adam were easily swayed because the enemy presented a half-truth, prompting the question: if part of it was true, then perhaps all of it was true. Coupled with the fear of missing out and how enticing the apple seemed, they couldn't resist the tempting bite... maybe God *was* holding out on them.

You and I are not that different from Adam and Eve though we have the lens of Jesus to filter the Bible through. The lies the enemy presents to us are so easy to agree with because sometimes we reinforce them with our thought paths. Picture a hiking trail or path in the woods on someone's old property: well-worn paths are recognizable and easy to pass through over and over again. They're familiar; perhaps they even feel safe. We can return to them, and we remember them well.

Like a road we've driven on to get home for years, we can pull into the driveway and realize we were driving the last five minutes and have arrived at our destination without thinking about it. These well-worn paths are easy, but when it comes to the lies we believe, these well-worn paths are detrimental to our souls.

Ask yourself: what is something you have been repeating in your mind that you can't believe you fell victim to? Did you get sucked into making a big purchase you really didn't need, and now you're kicking yourself over it? Or did you bite the lie that there's not enough out there for you, so you cut the corners to get ahead on a project to get a big promotion before so-and-so did, because if you didn't you might never get another chance? Or do you self-medicate each night because you can't stop ruminating on the thought that maybe you are living a lie? Maybe you *are* a terrible wife and mom. Maybe your husband *doesn't* love you after all.

Beloved friend, you will *maybe* yourself and your relationships to death if you don't stop walking these dangerous paths. Thought paths that you return to and trod over and over again will actually create neuropathways in your brain that feel true. Your brain and body were designed in such a way by your Creator God that you actually can renew your mind and take your thoughts captive to the authority of Jesus. You literally have the ability to renew your mind in an unhealthy or a healthy way simply by intentionally thinking about something over and over and over again.

This is why He tells us, "Fix your thoughts on what is true, and honorable, and right, and pure, and lovely, and admirable. Think about things that are excellent and worthy of praise" (Philippians 4:8 NLT). But here's the challenge—the enemy knows all of this, too.

He knows that your body is designed in such a way that he can use it against you. If he can whisper lies into your mind, continue to repeat them, help your brain look for things to validate them, and send things and people your way to provide just enough half-truth-evidence, then you will start believing they are true. You are essentially creating these pathways in your own mind—and, therefore, you have the power to stop. You also have the power to create new pathways. This is the science of rumination and the neuroplasticity of your brain.

Cogito, ergo sum (Latin for "I think, therefore, I am")—René Descartes.

Mind over matter.

We've heard these phrases or similar ones throughout our lives. If you've spent any amount of time in church, then you've heard things said about taking our thoughts captive to the authority of Christ. I've mentioned it here in this chapter already, but I'll say it again because it's important enough to reiterate: this is absolutely something we have the power to do. There is biblical and scientific truth to this practice.

You are creating neural pathways in your brain for things that you ruminate upon. Dr. Brooklyn Storme explains when we continue to think thoughts with enough regularity, they become clearer pathways for the brain, much like a new path you're breaking in. The more you walk the path, the clearer and more defined the path becomes, and it's easier to pass through and return to it.

During my research for this chapter, I found Dr. Storme's article and example resonated deeply with my own story. Growing up, I observed and learned that if you want anything in life, you have to work hard to get it. And the hard workers who put in the effort get the good things. Laziness gets you nothing and nowhere.

Without even realizing it, this attitude had become a core part of my beliefs: my efforts are what lead to positive rewards. As a single mom trying to work my way out of poverty, I put in long hours and sought to outwork my peers to stay ahead and become successful. It wasn't that I wanted to outdo *them*, I genuinely believed that if I worked hard enough, *someone* would notice and good things would come.

I exhausted myself in college in the evenings after work to achieve my degrees because I had heard most of my life that college helps get you out of poverty.

These are all good things inherently: to work hard, put forth your best efforts, and succeed. But they are at risk of being unhealthy things when they are at the expense of more important things, such as the simple practice of caring for this body the Lord has entrusted me with, which He refers to as the temple for His Holy Spirit. It becomes unhealthy if I begin to wrap up my identity in achieving these things. Neglecting to practice healthy disciplines means that I'm less healthy for my people as well.

Thankfully, God brought clarity to my mind and heart a few years ago when He called me to focus on studying rest and putting it into practice. I finally realized I didn't want to be on the exhaustion-badge-train anymore, no longer desiring to celebrate being busy. No longer wanting to applaud overworking and imbalance over a healthy and more boundaried lifestyle where work had appropriate edges that allowed me to be more present in my life outside of work.

Still, I had to constantly repeat my new belief. *Busyness is not better. Choosing rest is holy. Choosing rest is healthy. Choosing rest is necessary. I'm more effective in my work when I'm rested. My brain and body are in healthier states and perform better with rest.* These are the things that I repeated and played over and over again in my mind. And now, they're a path I can more easily tread through. I still have to intentionally return to these healthy paths, but they're easier to return to now and are a natural healthy place I love to land. I'm so thankful the Lord empowers us to renew our minds in the way He designed them!

Choosing Healthy Thought Patterns

Another interesting brain fact: things that you dwell upon and allow yourself to focus on can become truths in your life because you were looking for things to confirm it. You are telling your brain to look for agreements. This is called frequency illusion in psychology. Don't believe me? I have a fun example to share with you that maybe you have heard before.

Think about the last time you went to purchase a new-to-you vehicle. Once you decided that you wanted to get a Honda Accord (or whatever vehicle), I bet you suddenly started seeing that make and model everywhere. Did everyone suddenly go buy that car the night before? Of course not. However, it sure seems like it because you certainly didn't see all those Accords out there before.

What happened is simple: you told your brain to start looking for Honda Accords because suddenly they're important to you. And now, your brain is watching for them and bringing them into your conscious focus. *Oh there's an Accord—Amy will like that. Hey Amy— look! There's a red one, and silver, and black, and the white one you want with the pearly shimmer! Girl, they are e.v.e.r.y.w.h.e.r.e.! Go get you one!*

I'm being half-silly here, but I know you know what I'm saying. You're thinking of an example right now. Isn't it so wild how this happens?! But it's important to know that you are choosing the way you filter and frame your world. YOU are telling your brain what to let in and what to ignore. There's also a pesky thing called confirmation bias that is helping you find proof of your choice of filter everywhere.

Think of the last time you were having a bad day. Picture yourself at the start of that day all over again. Let's say you get a redo, but here's the important truth to have in mind: if you constantly complain about and dwell upon how bad your day is going, your brain will start to pick and choose things that confirm this as reality.

Will you dwell upon how bad your day is going? Telling everyone around you how bad it has been?

Or I hope you will choose to immediately apply a positive filter with this new truth in mind. Positive thinking is truly powerful. God designed us with a way to choose which focus our brains will look toward which means there's science behind Philippians 4:8!

In the NIV, it says *"Finally, brothers and sisters, whatever is true, whatever is noble, whatever is right, whatever is pure, whatever is lovely, whatever is admirable—if anything is excellent or praiseworthy— think about such things."* This verse is not coincidental. This verse is a promise from your Creator telling you how to help your brain bring in the true, good, and lovely things. If you dwell upon those things, your brain will look for and bring in things that affirm the beauty in your life all around you.

Maybe you think I'm too positive. I hear you. Though you may not know me personally, please know I am keenly aware that we live in a fallen and broken world, full of hard and heavy things that cannot go away just by thinking. Yes, we have an enemy who would love nothing more than to steal, kill, and destroy. And yes, he knows how our brains work as well.

He knows if he can send that fiery dart (Ephesians 6:16) of destructive thoughts into our minds, the accompanying reaction we're going to have is like a fertile ground, ready to trustingly receive the seeds of his lies. I'm aware of all of this—better yet, I'm aware that I get to choose where my thoughts remain. Gratefully aware!

You have the power and the ability to decide what you will do with every thought when it lands in your mind. You can ruminate on it and dwell upon it and look for things that confirm it and agree with it. And even if you don't like the thought, you have the power to make it as though it's true in your mind if you continue to feed the thought with your own streaming thoughts and the words you're speaking or hearing.

However, you also have the power to filter in truth and lovely, light-filled things! Let's choose our focus well! Look up and look out child of God, there is evidence everywhere of His truth in your life and all around you. You can focus on these things that bring life. Allow your mind's garden to be watered here, where the beauty and health reside. It's here that you can regain control of your thoughts and your life.

There is great joy and peace to be found when we center our hearts upon Jesus. Seeking emotional and spiritual well-being helps establish a firm foundation and can lead you down the healthy paths of hope, light, and life.

Picture your mind as a flourishing garden and Jesus as your gardener, His tender and intentional hands at work within you. Though you are surrendering to His hands, you still have a job to do as well. It is your responsibility to determine what seeds you will cultivate in your garden. What seeds will you water with your thoughts and words? What paths will you continue to tread over and over again? I hope you'll choose to water the right seeds and walk the paths of truth. May you have a well-watered mind with life-giving paths where only the seeds that honor God and bring life are allowed to dwell. And may the lies of Satan never take root.

Even though I feel overwhelmed

Prayerful Application

Explore these questions alone in prayer with the Lord, and feel free to explore them later with a small group of friends:

1. What are the thoughts/phrases/ideas you seem to repeat in your mind that create a storm within you? What are you thinking in the moments when you feel overwhelmed?
2. Are these lies from the enemy? Half-truths that feel true but aren't wholly true? Write down any lies you are noticing when you feel overwhelmed.
3. When you look at those lies on paper, are they the root? Ask yourself what other thoughts or fears are present that connect you to that lie. What does _____ mean to you? Continue to pray that the Lord gives you spiritual discernment and clarity around what the root is.
4. Sometimes, I find it helps to recognize the disproportionate response the lie is causing by asking, "What's the worst that will happen if _____ is true?"
5. Now that you know what you are wrestling with, ask the Lord to reveal to you what He says over you. What does the Bible say about these things? What verses can you repeat in your mind and heart when you hear these lies trying to enter?
6. What is a simple truth you can cling to and speak over your heart to remind yourself of the truth when the lie tries to enter? Perhaps it's an "even though . . . I will" statement? Complete this sentence and keep it with you: "Even though I'm feeling _____, I will choose to remember _____."

Chapter Two
Even though the world feels scary

How long, O Lord, must I call for help?
But you do not listen!
"Violence is everywhere!" I cry,
but you do not come to save.
Must I forever see these evil deeds?
Why must I watch all this misery?
Wherever I look,
I see destruction and violence.
I am surrounded by people
who love to argue and fight.
(Habakkuk 1:2–3 NLT)

As I write this, my world is in an uproar that seems to groan louder and heavier with each wave of news. As I mentioned before, I am both a military wife and mother, and world events impact us uniquely. In the times that our world feels as though it's spiraling toward war, I cannot watch the news; the inescapable weight is too much. I'll receive direct messages from various platforms asking how my son and husband are feeling about the unfolding events. I feel Habakkuk's words deep in my bones. I too have shouted and asked, *HOW LONG, Lord, must I wait!? HOW LONG until I see your goodness? Where is your victory? I can't see it. Where are you?!*

When I look upon all of the hard and heavy things for too long, I can become exhausted and emotionally heartbroken. Devastation seems to abound in the news and across social media accounts and can bleed into our conversations.

There is an infinite list of new reasons the earth continues to quake in our generation: pandemics and epidemics, wars, political unrest, social unrest, deaths, addictions, deceit, and so much more. It can feel alarming, like breaking open a massive tree trunk to reveal destructive decay underneath a false, healthy exterior. With the ability to consume global media at any turn, we can watch as evil triumphs around our world and down our streets.

Like Habakkuk, I feel surrounded by people who thrive in argument and debate. The brazenness behind people's online responses is alarming; it's as though the drive to proclaim one's offenses is greater than the remembrance that there are people with hearts and souls on the receiving end of those opposing screens.

Has this world always been so broken? Are we just now seeing the gravity of it because information is so accessible? Or, are these the last days, and we're racing toward the end of time when Jesus will return as He has promised? Read about history or read the Bible, and I trust you'll agree—there is evidence that this world has been devastatingly broken and scary throughout the ages.

No matter your age or story, I am confident if we were having coffee this morning, you could tell me of the difficulties you've witnessed in your time. However, this chapter isn't about belaboring the heaviness or giving glory to the difficulty. I share these heavy wonderings simply to acknowledge that our world is a mess and it has long been a mess. This place is so broken, so fragile, and so confused. Wickedness abounds and appears amplified because of the celebratory welcome it receives. We are deeply in need of a savior.

Our hearts are longing for an answer: how do we choose to hope when this world is so scary? Beloved in Christ—we put our eyes back upon our Father. I've always loved this portion of the song "Turn Your Eyes Upon Jesus" by Helen Lemmel:

> Turn your eyes upon Jesus
> Look full in His wonderful face.
> And the things of earth will grow strangely dim
> In the light of His glory and grace.

You cannot fix your eyes upon peace, hope, and light when gazing upon darkness. If you are turning your eyes away from the light of Christ and placing them constantly on the path that shouts the depth of the darkness, you will see, focus, and dwell upon that darkness. God has equipped us for the battles we face on this side of heaven. One way to choose to hope when your season is hard is to fight with your sword (the Word of God). There's a promise from the Bible I want you to memorize with me. It's one of my favorite verses, reminding me to return my heart and eyes to Peace Himself. I know the power it has brought to my spirit and my mind, and I want you to know that, too. Write it on a card or sticky note and set it out somewhere you frequently spend time so you can read and meditate on it until it's tucked deep into your heart:

> You keep him in perfect peace
> whose mind is stayed on you,
> because he trusts in you. (Isaiah 26:3)

Right here in the Bible God is telling us how to turn our eyes toward Him. He's promising that He will keep you in peace when your mind is steadied upon Him, staying on Him, focusing on Him, looking to Him . . . *because you trust in Him.* Don't miss the details in that brief yet mighty promise from God to you. He wants to keep you in peace. He wants you to know the fullness of a peace-filled mind when you're able to stay your mind on Him and trust Him.

This is an intentional practice, creating neuropathways as we discussed in the previous chapter. When your eyes are drifting to the hard and heavy things, acknowledge the feelings and the pull. Proclaim to yourself (out loud if you're able) this verse again. Recall and repeat stories of His faithfulness. Perhaps have coffee or lunch with a friend who will help you recall remembrances of His faithfulness in your life. Listen to worship music and sing along if you are able. Revisit an old journal where you've noted His goodness and provision.

Proactively steady your mind on Him, steady it upon His character and faithfulness. I promise you, from personal experience, your hope and faith will be renewed. You will experience His unexplainable peace when you remind your heart, mind, and soul of His goodness.

You may ask: how do I trust a God who I feel has abandoned this world to burn like wildfire? What kind of God would allow such pain? How can He be loving when there's so much depravity and evil flourishing? In a world where evil is celebrated and sold as entertainment?

There are a million tough questions we all have, things we long to understand. Is Jesus truly enough? Am I a weak or poor Christian because I have these confusions and doubts? Many of these hard questions are left unspoken, though keeping them locked away in silence is preventing us from processing them in a healthy way. Our doubts and inquiries are not better silenced.

No, beloved—your questions are welcome in the presence of the Almighty. He wants you. ALL of you.

> Come to Me, all you who labor and are heavy-laden *and* overburdened, and I will cause you to rest. [I will ease and relieve and refresh your souls.] (Matthew 11:28 AMPC)

It doesn't say, *come to me when you have your crap together. Come to me when you act like you believe in me. Come to me when you stop doubting you of little faith.* No! He said come to me all who are weary because HE is where your peace resides. HE is where your hope, life, light, and refreshment reside. And He wants you to come *in* your weariness.

God never asked you to be whole before He was willing to welcome you. The gospel shouts from God's infinite love to you: *you are not worthy, you cannot be worthy on your own accord—and so I made a way through Jesus! COME TO ME! I love you right now, right where you are and right as you are in your wrestling with sin-disease. YOU are mine; I've called you by name and I gave my son for you!* THIS is the good news of the gospel.

You cannot do anything to earn it. And according to Romans 8:35-39, nothing can separate you from His love—not even your doubts or wonderings. I have found that my questions in the middle of the hard and heavy things are how He helps me begin to till the dirt. He uses those sacred inquiries to dig down below the surface and reach past the dryness and barrenness of my deserts to open me up to His living waters.

Another interesting truth about our minds and bodies is that when we are depleted, we cannot self-manage our responses well. I'm keenly aware of this, and when I'm tired, I'm not a pleasant person. It pains me to admit it, but it's definitely true. We humans tend toward selfishness as a default, and we like what we like when we like it. The tension is tight within me if my resources are depleted. Much like a hot cup of fresh coffee in my hands, if someone bumps me, that molten hot reality of my feelings may spill out in these moments.

When my seventeen-year-old nephew died in a tragic accident, I was so angry with God and so confused by my anger. How could a loving God allow such a tragedy? I was wrestling with my own aching confusion as my beloved sister wielded her brokenhearted questions at me since I was a safe place for them to land. Though I feared I would crumble and respond poorly as the questions came, by the grace and kindness of the Holy Spirit alone, I was able to stay steady and not react in an effort to shut it down. I remain so grateful she shared those hard thoughts with me. Even as I recall being honored to hear her honest wrestling, I was completely lost on how to navigate the depth of our pain in the context of my faith in a God who I still believed was good.

I was angry and confused at God, too. I didn't understand how He could allow this. My friend Mande told me something that radically changed the way I understood God in my anger: "God can handle your anger, Amy. It's not your job to defend His character. He can handle your sister's anger, too." I cannot tell you how empowering and healing it was when I realized that God welcomed my anger and doubts. He wanted me to come and process the hurt with Him, even as I yelled my fears out at Him.

Like Habakkuk, He wanted me to come and pour out those challenging questions. I had vented to my husband, my girlfriends, my colleagues, seemingly any human that would listen—but had I taken it to Him yet? I don't know why, but it seemed like a foreign concept to go to Him with my questions, although it also made so much sense to run to Him with my hurt and inquiry.

When I ruminated on my pain and anger and talked it out with other people, I willingly kept my eyes on the darkness. But when I looked to God and brought that anger to Him—like Habakkuk—I left with praise on my lips. Even when my words were silenced by the weight of my unanswered questions, praise was somehow budding again in my heart. I can't explain it, but every single time I go to Him, I leave better and lighter because of His nearness. Through decades of living, I've learned that many of life's hard questions don't have answers neatly packaged or easily revealed. What better place to take those tangled, messy wonderings than to the one true source of hope, peace, and light?

When the Pain Is Close to Home

What about when things are way too close to home? When you don't feel heard in your struggle for answers about what's happening with your body, and then you finally arrive in the office of someone who will listen and they tell you those devastating words: *it's cancer*.

When you wonder if you're the reason people continue to leave because it seems you're the only common denominator, and it feels like broken relationships are your destiny.

When you've tried to have a baby for years and have so much debt and tears and hear yet again, *not pregnant*.

When your 17-year-old, beautiful nephew crashes his truck less than a mile from home one morning on the way to school and everything in your family's world crashes and halts because he died at the scene. As his little sister reels from the pain and confusion of having been tossed in the truck, too, but is still breathing—where is God then?

These are the questions my heart achingly asks. These are stories of people I deeply love, and some are stories of my own. I'm sure you have questions of your own as well, friend. How do I have "even though . . . I will" faith in the seasons where it feels as though nothing seems good in my world or when the darkness is drowning out the light?

This is definitely one of those tangled, messy questions. There may be no explanation on this side of heaven, but I have found some things that help me turn back toward the light in these heavy and dark spaces. One thing that helps me is knowing I'm not alone. Friendships and relationships are kindled when we hear those heavy, but uniquely comforting words *"me too."*

Katherine Wolf is a vibrant, beautiful woman with a story that both wrecks and inspires me. She coauthored a book titled *Hope Heals* with her husband Jay, where they tell their powerful story of God's faithfulness and how they found hope in their very hard story. I cannot recommend their inspiring book enough!

Katherine experienced a devastating medical event that nearly took her life, and it was just the beginning of a road of significant difficulty for her and her family. She and Jay reach thousands through their ministry Hope Heals with the truth that we can absolutely still have joy even in the middle of our suffering.

We all live daily within the mixture of good and difficult living; is there ever a day that goes by where everything is truly good? We can certainly choose to frame our world with a positive lens, to see the gifts in the moments. I intentionally practice this positive framing daily! However, it is also incredibly healthy and necessary to hold space for and allow your body, heart, and soul to process suffering and grief.

Where did we as a church get the idea that joy cannot coexist with sorrow? As I add days to my years, I'm learning that I can hold grief and joy in the same embrace. I can grieve the emotional loss of my precious father and beautiful nephew while also acknowledging the physical weight of the grief my body is experiencing. And there in this same embrace, I can hold near the memories and the gratitude of the joy we shared in the time we had. Even here, I can grieve how deep their absence is while still finding joy in celebrating life milestones and celebrations.

Joy does not exist outside of and exclusive of suffering. As Christians, we are taught and we know that the joy of the Lord is our strength (Nehemiah 8:10). And when we are grieving, crushed spirits with breaking hearts—there in the messy middle of these tangled moments—we find Him holding us close. He tells us in Psalm 34:18, "The LORD is close to the brokenhearted and saves those who are crushed in spirit" (NIV).

I picture myself as a young girl, terrified of something in the dark, and my Father lifting me up and into His arms, resting my tear-stained-cheeks to His chest . . . safe. If my joy comes from God and is exclusive of my circumstances, then I can find joy and peace in the middle of deep valleys or great pain. I have experienced this so authentically that people comment they don't understand how I'm handling things so well.

But I have also sat deep within my grief and heaviness, allowing my soul to cry an audible wail. There, too, I found people could be moved to desire a deeper walk with the Lord, inspired somehow by the vulnerable processing I was willing to express. This journey we are on is not about us nor our ability to do everything right. Someone else's ability to come to Christ is not fully hinging upon our ability to navigate life's struggles well.

What does the Lord require of you? To act justly, love mercy, and walk humbly (Micah 6:8). Nowhere in the Bible will you read: *suck it up and stop being a baby. You better act like everything is good, or they won't believe that I'm a good God. Stop being sad (or insert other emotion here).*

What you will find are countless scriptures sharing stories of heroes of the Bible lamenting, processing their grief as well as celebrating their joy. Habakkuk is a beautiful example. His world was incredibly scary, and when he cried out to God, questioning where in the world He was, his fear was amplified:

> O Lord my God, my Holy One, you who are eternal—
> surely you do not plan to wipe us out? (Habakkuk 1:12 NLT)

The Lord's reply in Habakkuk 2 is complicated but beautiful. God reminds Habakkuk that He will triumph over evil, and though things might look bad, evil is not winning and will not prevail. Justice was coming and was already in motion, so He closes His answer to Habakkuk with this: "But the Lord is in his holy temple; let all the earth be silent before him" (Habakkuk 2:20 NIV). His reminder to Habakkuk is that He still reigns, and the earth remains in submission to Him.

Habakkuk's reply in chapter 3 is to speak of God's power, justice, and might. He shares how he is choosing to trust in God despite his anguish and fear, declaring,

> *Even though* the fig trees have no blossoms;
> and there are no grapes on the vines;
> *even though* the olive crop fails,
> and the fields lie empty and barren;
> *even though* the flocks die in the fields,
> and the cattle barns are empty,
> yet *I will* rejoice in the Lord!
> *I will* be joyful in the God of my salvation!
> The Sovereign Lord is my strength!
> He makes me as surefooted as a deer,
> able to tread upon the heights.
> (Habakkuk 3:17-19 NLT, emphasis added)

Katherine Wolf found deep inspiration in Habakkuk's story, too. Following the nudge of the Holy Spirit, she wrote her story's version of this passage to cling to as a promise of *"even though . . . I will"* faith:

> *Though I cannot walk,*
> *And I am confined to a wheelchair;*
> *Though half of my face is paralyzed,*
> *And I cannot even smile;*

> *Though I am extremely impaired,*
> *And I cannot take care of my baby;*
> *Yet I will rejoice in the Lord,*
> *I will be joyful in God my savior!*[2]

When Healing Doesn't Come

> But the LORD said to Samuel, "Do not consider his appearance or his height, for I have rejected him. The LORD does not look at the things people look at. People look at the outward appearance, but the LORD looks at the heart." (1 Samuel 16:7 NIV)

We are not "less than" if we have an ailment that goes unhealed. Katherine is a mighty, vibrant, powerhouse of a woman, and her presence is not hindered by her physical restrictions. When I process this verse through the lens of physical ability, it appears that the greater importance to God is the heart. Perhaps He's most concerned with what our testimony is and how our soul is. Are you OK with the possibility that God may only heal your soul and your physical fight may remain?

I've battled celiac disease for most of my adult life, and there's no cure. It's small compared to Katherine's battle, but it doesn't lessen the difficulty and frustration this physical disability brings me. I wrestle with social anxiety and physical difficulties despite being incredibly careful with my diet. I must power through a host of symptoms while people look at me with no idea of this internal battle.

Katherine said something so incredibly profound during an interview that it still sticks with me today. She often encounters people wanting to pray for her healing, and it's truly a lovely and wonderful thing to offer prayer. In a bonus interview Louie Giglio included in his Audible version of his book *Don't Give The Enemy A Seat At Your Table*, he asked Katherine to describe how she responds to this common offer of prayer for her healing. She welcomes their prayer and directs them to pray for her heart because she battles sin just like the rest of us. She said, "I am so much more than my body; there's a soul inside of me, and don't miss that."[3] Yes! She's a soul, a heart, a mind, and a wonderfully radiant human!

What if we were to pause and allow our minds to comprehend that God's plans and ways really aren't always the same as ours? (Isaiah 55:8-9) What if the healing He has promised to give is defined in a way that's different from what we desired or hoped for? What if heaven is where our bodies are whole and the greater importance here on earth is our soul?

Sometimes our story of healing will bring others to Christ and point to His power, and we still get to see beautiful miracles today. I've definitely seen many healing miracles! However, I've also seen many people who did not receive a physical healing this side of eternity.

I lost my father to an aggressive cancer that took his life less than sixty days from when we learned the cancer was in his body. It was bewildering, and I am weeping again as I write this. I remember my dad also learning of his oldest sister's cancer just days before he himself landed in the hospital. Initially, he wouldn't tell her he was in the hospital, nor that he had learned he too was suddenly on a cancer journey (they battled different types). His choice of secrecy was because he couldn't bear the thought of being a source of pain for his precious sister. He wanted her to feel strong and clear so she could fight, and he feared the devastation of his news would cause her too much pain and possibly derail her focus. In his selfless refusal to tell her, he inspired others.

I remember my uncle (David) speaking at my father's funeral, mentioning how he saw Christ's selflessness within my father, in the tender way his brother-in-law Bill chose others over himself. My father was inspiring and reaching others in his suffering and later in his death, far more than he had been when in his healthy care-free state. His story of suffering provided him with a unique opportunity, and he allowed God to use him in such humbling ways.

My precious aunt Bunnie did eventually learn of my father's cancer while he was still living, and they were able to encourage each other along their journeys. It was precious and sweet and heartbreaking all at the same time. Though it was devastating to witness their once strong and vibrant bodies be whittled away by cancer, their journey through suffering inspired so many. How brave, beautiful, and loving they were!

Another inspiring story of someone walking through suffering is our beloved friend's mom, Teresea, whom I mentioned earlier; who had passed a couple of years before Daddy. It was my first close walk alongside someone experiencing parental loss, such a very difficult journey.

My husband and I loved Teresea dearly, and her final days were not easy. In the last few weeks of her time on earth, Teresea's body began to fail in heartbreaking ways. She had gone from being completely independent to losing her vision, ability to walk, and use of both arms. It was devastating to know that this precious, sweet woman was having to battle such difficulties; yet the beauty of it was that she was so full of peace. A woman with a million reasons to be angry with God was instead calling her beloved sons close and asking that they not be bitter toward our good, kind God.

We would sing her favorite hymns or play her favorite worship songs, or her family would read her the Word and watch with awe as peace would cover her, and she would rest. We believed in and prayed for a radical miracle as we began to realize that God's plan for healing Teresea might not be what we desired. One of her children told us that she had said to him in the hospital, "You don't want me to have to keep living in this old body, do you?"

Of course not, we wanted her to be her vibrant self again! To get up off that bed, *"talitha kum"* like Jesus spoke to the little girl in Matthew 5:41. We wanted to see Teresea be miraculously healed.

Where we find ourselves though, is leaning into His kindness and peace as we wrestle out the sorrow of life without Teresea. Life without my father and my aunt. God is good. God is kind. Teresea is fully healed. My father is fully healed. My aunt Bunnie is fully healed. All three are vibrant, alive in heaven, and in the arms of Christ. And our hearts remain here tethered to this mortal world, still healing.

When we are walking through or walking alongside others as a loved one is passing, our "even though . . . I will" faith can sound something like, *"even though ____ is experiencing this tragic passing* *away of their body, we will rejoice in the Lord, in the God of our salvation, the only one who gives us strength and comfort for the days ahead when we will live without their wonderful presence here. You are good, God. Even here."*

When Words Fail

Loss is so hard. Facing suffering is so hard. Sitting in the brokenness of this world with mortal bodies can be devastating at times. It is here in this tension of hope and reality that sometimes fellow Christians say things we think are wise but are actually quite cutting, and deeply so. Things like, "God needed him more than we did. At least he's no longer suffering. He's better off than all of us having to still be here in this crazy world."

These are actual things I've heard in the wake of a loved one's passing. We wound people when we place our confusion and misunderstanding of God and prayer upon them with such platitudes. It's as though we think the power of prayer is based on our ability to believe or pray hard enough when perhaps we don't understand the depth and power of a gospel-awakened life, walking with Christ.

A gospel-awakened life is one that is aware of the gift of Jesus's infinite grace and centered on allowing His transformation in our hearts, minds, and spirits. Prayer is so much more than words repeated or craftily spoken in some formulaic exchange.

Many years ago, when my uncle Fred was dying of cancer, I actually had a woman in the church say to me that his death was imminent because we weren't believing enough for his healing. A man wholly devoted to Jesus whose last words on this earth were, "I love Jesus, I just love Jesus," moments before he faced his Savior in eternity, fully "alive" and cancer-free. It confused me and hurt me deeply as a new Christian.

I learned over time that she was misguided and didn't understand the fullness and kindness of God's presence that goes with us when we walk through suffering. Though it is a difficult truth to embrace, suffering is a guaranteed part of our life story.

Of course, faith is important. But God is all-powerful and all-mighty, and sometimes the healing we picture or want doesn't come according to our plan. Or it doesn't come without interventions from clinical experts. Or sometimes God does a far greater work through our suffering than we could've ever seen out of a swift miracle. Work we continue to see achieved through the beautiful ministry of Jay and Katherine Wolf and Hope Heals. As we saw in my father. And Teresea. In the seemingly most broken parts of their stories: they made the greatest kingdom impacts.

I love the AMPC version of John 6:12, Jesus specifically tells the disciples to gather up the broken fragments so that nothing is wasted—and I believe it's because Jesus wastes nothing. He specializes in using brokenness. So grateful.

Choosing Joy in Suffering

This life is good and this life is hard. Some seasons are good and some seasons are hard. Your joy is not exclusive of your pain or suffering. You can embrace grief and joy in the same embrace. Suffering and celebration can coexist in the same moments. Good and hard are not exclusive of one another. We can hope even when hope seems lost because our hope is eternal and in Christ and not in our circumstances or our outcomes.

Teresea's, my dad's, or even Katherine's story might feel more extreme than yours, but you are human and undoubtedly have wounds and spaces that need healing. Even if you have no impaired features, you may smile minimally or think of yourself as less lovely than you truly are.

YOU are created in the image of God (Genesis 1:27), crafted perfectly and intentionally by Him (Psalm 139:13-14). Every inch of your face and every minute of your story is beautiful, even the hard and heavy parts.

In my story, I found myself a college dropout, an abandoned single mama, a survivor of emotional abuse, and soon to be divorced from my first husband. Feeling trapped in debt, with many of my belongings repossessed, and with my heart shattered on the floor. Here I was, only a few short months into my Christian journey. Circumstances that could have caused me to throw in the towel instead rooted me so deeply into an awareness of Christ's love that my faith became unshakable.

God's infinite love and the promise that I would see His goodness because His Word would not return void (Isaiah 55:11, Psalm 27:13-14) was the life moving me forward. Now, over twenty years later, He has allowed me to use my story to breathe hope, light, and life into so many women wrestling their own hard stories similar to my own. Even the broken, fragmented places of my journey have been able to bring hope of joy to those who thought all was lost; there's the beauty of that verse coming to life again (John 6:12 AMPC). Jesus wastes nothing. Your story matters, dear one.

Something else I find special about Katherine Wolf's testimony is how she celebrates and proclaims how her journey is not God's back up plan. She believes that this is His story for her and her family.[4] I believe that because they've embraced this story and asked God how to steward their days, they have been entrusted with the platform they have. Hope Heals is a ministry that shares a message of hope with thousands daily.

Perhaps, like me, your story doesn't have such a large platform. Your testimony still matters deeply to those God has waiting to hear your words and see your smile and honest tears. You are not here by happenstance. And your journey is not accidental. I've learned firsthand that with God nothing is wasted. He wants every bit of you and your story, and He's ready to use it for your good and His glory (Romans 8:28, Genesis 50:20).

I'm praying for you today that you will trust God with all of you. Your anger, fear, joy, struggle, and sadness—every part of you. That your heart and eyes would open to the story He's weaving around you. May you be brave and share your story and see His goodness here, now. I hope you too will learn you can absolutely hold grief and joy in the same embrace.

Prayerful Application

Explore these questions alone in prayer with the Lord, and feel free to explore them later with a group of friends.

1. What is something hard that you are currently wrestling with in your life?
2. What, if anything, has caused you to be angry with God or to doubt God's goodness? Who could you safely talk to about it? (Someone who would help you filter it through the lens of the gospel and the Bible.) Where and when will you set up a time to talk with them? (Go send that text or email request now, friend.)
3. What are two verses that you would like to note from this chapter as ones you wish to memorize? Take a moment to view them in multiple Bible versions (or your version of choice). Put them on a sticky note or notecard and place it somewhere you will see it often.
4. Complete this sentence in the context of your answers to the above questions and keep it with you: Even though _____, I will choose to _____ .

Chapter Three
Even though I feel alone

My soul, wait only upon God
and silently submit to Him;
for my hope *and* expectation
are from Him.
(Psalm 62:5 AMPC)

The Commonality and Problem of Loneliness

Sometimes I feel so lonely. I've learned many of us battle feelings of loneliness; it is an incredibly common experience. It's reported that 40 percent of people are estimated to experience loneliness, and 60 percent of them are married.[5]

I would argue those numbers are even higher. Our feelings of loneliness are very much tied to our subjective experiences—how we feel that the quality and connection is with ourselves and others and if we feel disconnected. Social media actually heightens these feelings, too.

I don't have to present intensive research to you about that fact either. Those of us who use social media have experienced the sting of a friend group sharing their fun outing—when we were never invited.

Or the post where the couple continues to seem terribly perfect, as we hold our eye rolls and our spouses pass gas across the room. *(Letting you in on a little secret: science tells us that Mr. and Mrs. Perfect pass gas and roll their eyes, too . . . ☺)*

This chapter has nothing to do with demystifying or reducing loneliness because it is so common. Instead, this is more about acknowledging loneliness as a very real difficulty. When we find ourselves in a social-desert season, it can feel as though we are desperate for the comfort of companionship. We must ask: Is it possible that we can find ourselves well-watered in these desert seasons?

While writing the first segment of this book, both my son and my husband were away for military orders. My son is stationed in another country for 3-5 years, and my husband was on a temporary assignment seven hours from home for twelve months. I work from home primarily, which can be isolating, and my family of origin lives over an hour away with schedules that often can't align.

I have some family members I truly miss though I have to keep healthy boundaries with them, even as I long for an ideal that will never exist.

I work full time and volunteer in my church.

I have two small groups I meet with monthly and two best friends that I can't see near enough because of distance or life seasons.

I work in a very public role at my large employer and meet a ton of people regularly.

I have nine social media accounts, of which I'm frequently active on five.

I am sharing all this to explain that I have a network of people around me and even with all of that—I wrestle with bouts of loneliness.

How can I have so many people around me and still feel so lonely at times? How can you too have a social media presence, a family or neighbors, church, or work connections and also battle loneliness? Sometimes we wrestle with loneliness despite being surrounded because the quality and depth of relationships are not what we expected.

A wild truth that Dr. Winch shares in his article is that thinking about past loneliness increases our perception of loneliness in our current state.[5] This is further evidence of the incredible power of our minds, especially when it comes to what we ruminate on.

Loneliness is a very real difficulty, but there are things we can do to wrestle out of the pit that loneliness attempts to hold us deep within. One such thing is remembering the power God has given us to remain in control of our thought patterns.

Another is to be purposeful in prayer over our connections, and actively build healthy relationships. This can be as simple as praying for the Lord to reveal to you whom you should focus and invest your time and energy with. And then be intentional in connecting with them. Practically speaking this is as simple as sending them a text to check in when they come to mind. Invite them to coffee or lunch or another thing you might enjoy together. Relationships require time and energy.

We can't deeply connect with everyone in our lives, but we should all be nurturing a deeper friendship with someone. So, who is the Lord calling you to nurture a more focused, deeper connection with? Listen. And then take action as the Holy Spirit leads.

Friendships Lost Due to Change in Proximity (Changing Churches, Jobs, Cities)

After ten years in the same church, God led my husband and me away to search for a new church home. Before moving ahead with the decision, we spent months in prayer, fasting and talking it out often with each other. We processed with wise people we respected, all while seeking the Lord's guidance. The most difficult part of that obedient yes for me was the impact it would have on my friendship circle.

Several years earlier, I had been deeply aware of how lonely I was. I had lots of friends and lots of acquaintances, but no true confidants. No one knew the deep thoughts, dreams, hopes, sorrows, and wonderings of me. And there was no one I could be such a shoulder for in return. Nearly all of my connections were surface level, and I was drowning in the shallow depths of loneliness. I remember praying that God would bring me a friend or friends I could go deeper with.

Friends I could lock arms with and be truly vulnerable with. I longed for a connection with depth.

My husband and I are so blessed to enjoy friendship with one another. But he cannot be expected to successfully wear the hat of being a good girlfriend to me. It's healthy and good to have a safe friend you can process life with, and if you're married, I mean in addition to your spouse. God had opened my eyes to this relational need. And over time, He blessed me with wonderful friendships and mentors.

I was intentional about nurturing these relationships for years, so when my husband and I realized God might be calling us away from the church community we shared—my heart shattered. I'm not exaggerating when I share that I placed my face to the floor with hot pouring tears, begging God to change His mind and my husband's mind (on multiple occasions during our months of seeking clarity). How could good come from this? Both God and my husband seemed very clear that we were being guided away, and I was so afraid to accept it.

My heart-cries sometimes sounded like this: God, it took years to build these friendships! When we're no longer in proximity, they'll forget me! They'll stop inviting me, they'll fill their circle with someone new!

I'm sure I shouted or whispered other tear-filled sorrows as I processed the truth that I knew in my heart: God really was calling us away. And truly more than my comfort, I do want God's will. But it doesn't mean it's easy to follow when it feels like there's so much to lose.

As I embraced the reality ahead of us, I remember Exodus 33:15 was a prayer of my heart, "... if your Presence does not go with us, do not send us up from here" (NIV). Followed closely by verse 16 "How will anyone know that you are pleased with me and with your people unless you go with us? What else will distinguish me and your people from all the other people on the face of the earth?" (NIV).

I asked God to prepare my heart for this change and to hold me through it if it was His will, and He was so faithful to do exactly that. In His kindness, He gave me wisdom on how to be intentional in our exit so I could nurture friendships with purpose. He was my courage as I trusted Him with what was to come.

My friendship circle has definitely changed and many of those friendships have been dramatically altered, casualties of proximity that no longer exists. But God was faithful to hold me every single step of the way. Though I continue to experience changes in my circle, I'm so grateful that we were obedient and said yes to what God was calling us to. That "yes" has led me to countless things that never would've transpired if I had stayed in the comfort of the familiar.

Our "yes" has allowed me to meet people whom God has used powerfully in my spiritual development; people I never would have crossed paths with otherwise. My husband and I are being nourished spiritually in ways our hungry souls didn't realize they were yearning for. God has increased our spiritual intimacy as a couple in magnificent ways.

We've seen close friends' families flourishing who visited our new church; a church that's now theirs, too.

Within this new community, I found the wisdom and courage to walk an individual therapy journey where I learned places my heart needed mending. I've gone deep with new women God wanted my soul to connect with whom I never would've met if I had played it safe. I've experienced many sorrows with this journey, too, but none of them are worth more than the peace of knowing I'm exactly where God wants me to be.

At some point in your journey, beloved, God will call you to something new, and you may fear the impacts it will bring to your friendship circle, too. You may find yourself in such a season right now where God is about to move you or your family in a big way. Perhaps a new city? Perhaps a new job or a new church? Whatever your next season looks like, I am praying that you will embrace your good God's good plans for you and your life. His goodness is not contingent upon your comfort. But rest assured, loved one, whatever He has planned for you is greater than anything you could hope for or plan for yourself. And the Comforter Himself will hold you through it all; He is faithful. And He is faithful to you.

When Friends No Longer Choose You

What about when friends no longer choose you? How does one process the sting of being rejected, or never embraced? I have been both the one rejected, and it pains my heart to admit it, but also the rejector. Please don't close your book yet—hear me out as I explain some science behind this and a possible "why" for someone who doesn't accept an invitation to go deeper in friendship.

Sometimes we are in seasons of life where we just don't have the capacity for anything extra, including additional people, and it is a very healthy thing to have that level of awareness. As I previously shared, one of the wrestlings I've been working through in therapy is my need to please others. And part of the journey of healing is realizing that it is important to define who is important to me so that I can be purposeful in making space for them (and to care well for myself, too).

My therapist led me to complete a concentric circle exercise. According to psychologist and anthropologist Robin Dunbar, famous for his research on relationships and "Dunbar's number," we can only adequately maintain and give the time necessary to nurturing around five "shoulders-to-cry-on" friendships and around fifteen total core social partners.[6]

For explanation's sake, friendship circles are expressed as concentric circles where the center is labeled intimates (think your spouse/significant other), then close friends, best friends, good friends, friends, acquaintances, and known names. As a result, when my "close friends" circle and "best friends" circle are already healthy and full, I can't continue to add more without taking away precious time from the others I'm already deeply connected with.

This means when a beautiful, wonderful person wants to go deeper than being only a friend or even a good friend—it's a risk that might land in rejection. And it hurts my heart to say it—but—this has certainly happened. I've had to say no, so that I can guard time with my husband who for much of our marriage had traveled often for the army (including deployments) and sometimes was only home for short windows of time.

I've had to say no to an offer to hang out so that I can keep space open for my closest friends because I'm already committed to a friend coffee or want to keep the space open for connecting with them over text or a call. I've had to say no to incredibly wonderful people so that I could keep time free for a day to care well for my mind, body, and soul through what I affectionately call a "me day." Even extroverts need days to unplug from social connections and rest in the presence of God in whatever way it needs to look like on our own "me" day.

I am sharing all this to explain that while there are unhealthy people out there who hurt others with ill intentions, it is often not that the person who hasn't accepted your invite has ill will toward you. It is likely that perhaps it is not the right season for this particular connection to go deeper.

God has shown me time and again that He is faithful in my relationships as I've prayed and allowed Him to lead. And He's also shown me great comfort when I realized I needed to stop wrestling with sorrow over someone who didn't reciprocate my interest in building a connection. It's after those moments of heart-healing that I am able to look up and around and nurture the healthy relationships that I'm being called to. I don't know about you, but I would much rather have 2-5 authentically deep close friendships, than many shallow-depth friend connections.

Perhaps for you, your challenge is not that you are longing for more friendships but that you are saddened because the ones you have are fading. It's difficult to experience friendships waning. When this happens, it can be helpful to pray and ask the Lord to show you why. Asking Him to reveal the why could help you see if you have any control or influence over it. A thing about control and influence is this: *if you have no role—then you definitely have no control.* But if you can see where you have a possible role, then your ability to influence change is regained. It is brave and good to look inward. I can only control myself, my thoughts, and my actions. Therefore, I think it's important to always look inward and practice self-awareness and self-management.

Here, this looks like practicing honest objectivity and asking yourself: Am I being a good friend? Am I being purposeful in connecting with my friends, praying for them, reaching out to them, and honoring any difficult seasons they are wrestling with? One could certainly belabor any weaknesses they appear to bring to the friendship, but loved one—you are the one reading this book right now. So, I want to challenge you to consider what only you can control (your choices).

You can choose to be brave and consider if you may have a role in this shifting friendship dynamic. If the answer is yes, you can begin to put words and actions to what might be needed to influence your friendship positively. Sometimes, because of the busyness of life, we can get distracted from nurturing good things. Things like exercise, houseplants, and friendships. It's important to recognize when this happens and begin blocking time for these very good things again. Prayerfully asking God to show you your role in the waning of your friendship is an invitation for Him to search your heart and help you grow. I have long loved to echo this prayer from David, "Search me, O God, and know my heart! Try me and know my thoughts! And see if there be any grievous way in me, and lead me in the way everlasting!" Psalm 139:23-24.

Whether you are feeling alone because you don't have a strong friendship to nurture or because your friendships have faded, this truth applies. Dearly loved daughter of God, He desires for you to be in fellowship and relationship with Him and with others. I know He will fulfill this longing of your heart that aligns with His desires for you. Will you trust God to lead you to the right friendships? Will you pray and welcome Him to connect you with the exact friendship circles He wants to plant you within so that you flourish? Will you trust Him in the pruning as old friendships fall away or unhealthy ones fade?

I promise you from a heart of hope and a life of experience—He has consistently answered my prayers for friendship and sisterhood in every phase of my life. He is faithful; invite Him into this deep part of your heart's desires. Invite Him to lead you and help you connect with the exact right women He desires to connect you with. And lean into Him as you naturally grieve doors that close and doors that never opened.

Intentionality in Fighting Loneliness Through Building Friendships

I'd love to introduce you to someone I know whom we'll call Sally. Obviously, her real name isn't Sally, but you don't need to know her personally to connect with her story.

Sally is in a challenging season of life. She's suddenly found herself alone, realizing that she has not nurtured friendships outside her family members. Now that her children have grown up and flown the nest, she has become more aware of her current friendship state.

Her husband works and has additional responsibilities; this leaves her with a lot of time to herself. Sally does not currently work outside the home, serve in a local church, or have other community involvement. She's cordial with her neighbors and others when attending church, but only sees those individuals when she is in proximity to them. Her church primarily gathers once weekly, so she only spends seconds to minutes near those individuals each week, leaving only enough room for small talk or greetings and salutations.

Her interactions with her neighbors are a wave or brief hello near the mailboxes or when bumping into each other while running errands. Sally is lonely and isn't able to connect with her family frequently either, usually due to lack of proximity or busyness.

Do you know a Sally? Is God calling you to befriend a Sally? Are you a Sally?

Here's the thing about relationships: they require time, proximity, and prioritization. It is never too late to start building a friendship or network of friends. Still, if you do not make an effort to put yourself out there in the world to meet people and get to know those around you, you will for sure remain lonely. What does "putting yourself out there" look like for you in your current season? Could it mean getting a part-time job? Volunteering in a local organization or with your church ministry? Inviting some neighbors or church acquaintances for a weekly or bi-weekly walk? Attending a neighborhood potluck or community event?

A wonderful strategy, too, is to ask the Lord to tell you who to reach out to and invite them to coffee. The first step beyond praying is to take action and put yourself in proximity to others with the purposeful intention of getting to know them. What if we're all waiting for the other person to make the move to start the conversation? What if you moved past your fears of rejection, feeling awkward, or whatever other feeling is holding you back, and you just invited the first three people who come to your mind right now for one-on-one coffee or tea? They might say no. And . . . they might say yes. You might find that you both loved connecting over coffee or tea, and you schedule another and another, and suddenly you're deepening a friendship that may have never happened if one of you didn't offer the first "let's hang out!"

It's also possible you might find that there's no connection. No matter the outcome, it's worth the stretch to invest in your relationships and connections. Go be brave!

Perhaps you're nervous or unsure of how to connect because you've been focused on your family for so long that you're not sure how to create new friendships. If that's you, I'd love to share a few practical tips for connecting:

1. It's so effective that it's worth repeating: pray about who, and then invite them. I promise you the Lord will help lead you if you invite Him to. It may simply be a few names that pop into your mind as you're thinking and praying, or perhaps someone you can't get off your mind. Trust those thoughts. I've found it's so often His gift of knowledge. It may be a singular connection or a friendship in the making.
2. Communicate timely, and be on time when you meet. This shows the other person they matter enough that you are making them and this connection a priority.
3. Learn how to pronounce their name, and use it when talking. Research proves that saying someone's name when communicating increases bonding.
4. Be a great listener. Being heard is a powerful gift you can give your new friend. Share parts of your story,

too. But take caution to not dominate the conversation. I admit, I have avoided people who drain me and don't seem to care about knowing me.
5. While connecting, continue to ask questions to get to know them and listen to their responses without diving in with long details of your own stories that derail their flow. Think of this like a gentle back-and-forth, and trust the flow. You will have your chance to share, too, but let them finish their pieces. And if you don't get your chance or discern they aren't interested in knowing you, it's OK to privately pray and consider whether this connection is meant to continue or not.
6. Reciprocate intimacy as you are comfortable. If the person shares a prayer request, consider sharing one, too. If they tell you tough parts of their story, if you're ready, share some deeper details of your story, too. Again, honor the flow, take care to ensure they feel heard, and look for signs that you are welcome to feel heard, too.

You cannot nurture friendships that don't yet exist. Inviting someone into a relationship is a risk because it's possible that you may get rejected. However, if you do not make any attempts to widen your circle, then you are guaranteed to remain in your current state.

I have a decorative sign in my office at work that says it simply: if nothing changes, nothing changes. Beloved, if you change nothing, then your lack of relationships is also likely not to change. Are you willing to ask yourself what your role might be in this season of loneliness? Is it time to be brave? Is it time to be willing to put yourself first occasionally so you can be healthy for others as you receive the life-giving nourishment that comes from having healthy close friendships?

God designed us to be in relationship with others. We need each other. And no one person can carry the weight of being everything we need: Jesus alone carries that title. All the humans in your life have smaller (wonderfully lovely) purposes.

Your spouse is not your savior and could never be your peace or complete you. I used to love that line from the movie Jerry Maguire when he says, "You complete me"—teen-girl-me swooned at the thought of being whole once I met my person (major eye roll happening here now). Much more mature and (ahem) slightly older me realizes that the only one who can complete me is God.

The people in my life He gifts me with have specific gifts and roles, and not one of them is meant to be all things. My husband is my most intimate partner who gets the deepest parts of me at every level of intimacy (spiritual, emotional, physical, and so on). My close friends are who I call upon (and am available to) when the world feels as though it's crashing, or I need solid, Spirit-led, and prayer-covered advice (and all the wonderful, good things, too)! I fight loneliness by letting them in when I feel overwhelmed or unseen.

I'm blessed to know a few sacred others I love to spend time with, grow deeper with, and share parts of myself with that no one in any outer circle gets to know. These girlfriends are sacred sisters . . . soul sisters if you will. I can process emotional, spiritual, and other honest wrestlings with them differently than I would with my husband, my family, and anyone else.

These soul sisters are a priceless gift from God Himself. They challenge me to go deeper with God, seek to be healthy, to love my husband and family well, and to show up and love them (my soul sisters) well, too. They know my hopes and throw kerosene on the sparks of my dreams. They pour water on the embers of my fears and silence the lies of the enemy by reminding me of the truth in God's Word. They hold me accountable and hold me when I fall. They're worth every single hard-fought second that we've invested in befriending one another. Soul sisters are worth it, friends. Pray to know who yours are, build and nurture those connections—and cherish them.

Prayerful Application

Explore these questions alone in prayer with the Lord, and feel free to explore them later with a small group of friends:

1. Describe where you are when it comes to feelings of loneliness.
2. How is your relationship with God? How is your relationship with your spouse or significant other? How is your relationship with your immediate and extended family?
3. Google concentric circles to understand the visual diagram as well as the contents. Then practice writing out what yours looks like. What's your greatest need right now as you look at your circle on paper? Do you need to create more margin or create more connections?
4. Would you consider yourself a good friend? Why or why not? If you think yourself a good friend, what do you do well? If you think of yourself as a not-so-good friend, what could you do better? Note: if you're exploring this question in a group setting, pause, pray, and take caution to answer with honesty and humility. Take at least 2-3 minutes in silence to dwell on this question before you answer together.
5. What's one thing you're going to do today or this week to act on what you've learned in this chapter?
6. What is a simple truth you can cling to and speak over your heart to remind yourself of God's faithfulness in your current season? Bible verse? An "even though . . . I will" statement? Complete this sentence and keep it with you: "Even though I feel alone, I will choose to remember ____."

Chapter Four
Even though there are no answers

Why, O Lord, do you stand far away?
Why do you hide yourself in times of trouble?
(Psalm 10:1)

How Can I Choose to Hope When All I See Is the Unknown?

Easing north around the gentle curve leading out of Helen, Georgia back to our mountain cabin rental, my phone began to frantically alert me that I had missed several calls and texts due to the lack of cell signal within the tiny mountain town. Ping, ping, ping! Voicemails and texts were flooding in from my father, my aunt, and his girlfriend. Something was clearly wrong, each message said to call back as soon as possible.

I called my father first and learned he had collapsed that morning and was being loaded into an ambulance for transport from the limited services regional hospital in his small town to a larger city hospital for immediate care. My heart sank and my stomach churned as tears and fear welled up within me. My dad was in Florida, and I was many hours away in North Georgia.

My husband and I reside in southeast Tennessee but were out of town for a desperately needed weekend getaway. I hadn't slept at all the night before because we thought our dog would do OK without a crate overnight during our trip. We were definitely mistaken, our dog is absolutely a creature of habit and was restless, moving about our room the whole night without having his crate to retreat to (we now have a travel crate that works like a charm).

Due to a lack of sleep, I was in no shape to drive, so we made the hard yet wise decision to stay the final night and get some rest before going home and then diving into whatever unknown was ahead of us. I prayed hard and called upon prayer warrior friends and loved ones to pray too. My mind raced constantly. Do I rush to Florida tomorrow to be with Daddy or wait to learn what's going on first?

I was in my first year at a new job after leaving a career of more than sixteen years at my prior organization. I didn't have the banked leave hours to be off, but I thankfully had the flexibility to temporarily work remotely in another state with leader approval so that I could at least be nearer to my dad in this uncertainty. So, with my manager's permission, as soon as we were home the next morning (a Sunday), I showered, packed fresh clothes, and hit the road for the nine-hour drive to get to the hospital where my dad was. I can't explain how I knew, but I knew I had to be there. Something very big was going on, and the Lord was lovingly letting me know that my dad needed me. Heavy with both peace and anguish, I hurried to his side.

We waited in the unknown for a few days. It was a holiday weekend and key specialists weren't going to be at the hospital until Tuesday. Sunday to Tuesday was painstakingly long. The unknowns were flooding our minds, and I was feeling overwhelmed by my own perceived need to carry the emotional weight of my father and his girlfriend. I am highly empathetic, and I feel deeply what I imagine and recognize others may be feeling in addition to my own feelings.

My father was trying to appear confident and OK, but I knew him, and he was scared. His girlfriend was too. She loved him, and the waiting and worry of possible cancer was difficult for her as well.

For all of us. Sometimes in the unknown, we may withdraw, or we may process our fear out loud with others. My father was the former, and his girlfriend was the latter. She truly meant well, but she asked me some hard questions I wasn't quite ready for.

Will he die?

Is he saved?

Difficult questions to ask a daughter who is trying to hold onto hope that her father is going to be OK, and we had no answers about what was going on inside his body.

I responded with kindness and grace as best as my breaking heart was able since I trusted her questions came from a place of love. Finally, the time came to do the MRI to learn if he had cancer. The hours that followed felt like weeks. We asked repeatedly when the hospitalist would be by to tell us the results. No answers. No clarity. It felt like we were being avoided, and I assure you I am a very positive person—for me to say that means it truly was reality.

Finally, a specialist helping do rounds made the bold decision to tell us the results. She was no longer going to let us wait; thank you Jesus for people with compassion and empathy!

She shot us straight. It's cancer. She began to read off bewildering details and numbers and descriptions; my head was spinning, and my father hung his head so very low.

She left the room, and I rushed to his bedside and held him as he began to weep. My six-foot-three, larger-than-life, strong, and fiercely independent daddy wept at the news that he had cancer. It was September 2nd when he went to the emergency room in his small Florida town and September 5th when he was diagnosed.

We navigated a host of unknowns through the journey that followed. Twists and turns, hope springing forth one moment and dashed possibilities the next. It was every bit of the rollercoaster I've heard people describe cancer journeys to be.

On November 2nd my father took his final breath while holding my hand and squeezing it one last time with the last ounce of strength he had. My heart still aches as I remember feeling his heart stop beating underneath my other hand. I'll never not hurt when I think about his treacherous journey with cancer, the swiftness of it all, and the suddenness of his loss.

Nothing was clear in that season. Every single day was full of unknowns, though a true constant that remained near was Christ. I saw Jesus woven into the journey every single step of the way. It is the only thing that kept me from crumbling under the weight of this heavy season.

Navigating the Unknown: Waiting Well

If there's anything my innumerable walks through the unknown have taught me, it's that they are a guarantee of this life. The only predictable thing about the unknown is we will all walk through such seasons. I have lived in faith communities where it was the "Christian" thing to do to not admit "negative" emotions. It's as if you were speaking ill over yourself if you admitted the reality of hard emotions. That is not biblical! Paul teaches us in Romans 12 that we should weep with those who weep, not snap them out of their feelings and tell them to look to happy stuff.

It is absolutely normal and OK to both have faith and feel fear and confusion as you face the unknown. I can believe God is good and able to bring a miracle while acknowledging the sadness and fear I'm feeling. Grief and joy can be held in the same embrace just like faith and fear. In fact, courage is the choice to move forward despite the feelings of fear. To keep breathing, keep living, keep hoping even when earthly things tell us it's dire. We can feel all those things while still choosing to look to and cling to hope for the good and miraculous. The Bible speaks of numerous encouragements to help us navigate seasons of confusion and difficulty. A few verse examples include:

> Rejoice in hope, be patient in tribulation, be constant in prayer. (Romans 12:12)

> Do not be anxious about anything, but in everything by prayer and supplication with thanksgiving let

your requests be made known to God. And the peace of God, which surpasses all understanding, will guard your hearts and your minds in Christ Jesus.
(Philippians 4:6-7)

Even though I walk through the valley
    of the shadow of death,
I will fear no evil,
for you are with me;
your rod and your staff,
they comfort me. (Psalm 23:4)

In speaking of every dire thing that he sees occurring around him and still not knowing the outcomes ahead, Habakkuk chose to rejoice in what he knew to be true of the Lord. He goes on to say, "yet I will rejoice in the LORD; I will take joy in the God of my salvation" (Habakkuk 3:18).

Countless times throughout his writing in the Psalms, King David took his thoughts and heartache and honestly poured them out to the Lord. One such example is Psalm 13, and often like in this Psalm, he ended with reminding himself to hold onto hope "But I have trusted in your steadfast love; my heart shall rejoice in your salvation. I will sing to the LORD because he has dealt bountifully with me" (Psalm 13:5-6).

There are many timeless examples throughout the Bible of people walking through incredible difficulty and vast unknowns. I am so grateful those stories are not all tied neatly with a pretty bow and presented piously or with perfection. Instead, they are honest renderings of humans navigating dark and hard things. And sometimes sucking at it. And sometimes doing decent, sometimes being extraordinary, and always when something beautiful was coming from it—it was evident that beauty was rooted in the Lord.

I've found in my own personal journey that in every difficulty and unknown I've faced, the one true, steady constant that gave me light and life and hope was Christ. He is the only one who has helped me remain steady in a world that is anything but steady. But it's not always evident. Usually, I have to get quiet and be still in order to see

Him and know He is near and in it with me. And when I'm failing at that quietness and stillness, it is almost always because I'm trying to survive this "thing" in my own strength. I'm spinning plates wildly and striving and doing and exhausting my body, mind, and spirit. Until I allow myself to either collapse or become aware of that self-striving and get it back in check, I'll remain in utter internal chaos.

In these moments, I'm hypersensitive and my emotions are on edge. Like those silly emotions characters in the movie *Inside Out* circling wildly around their command center seemingly out of control, I picture that's what my mind looks like in such times.

But! When I can quiet my soul and get still and look to Jesus, I can't fully describe what it does for me. It really is a peace that surpasses understanding as Philippians 4 describes. That peace comes from Him, not me. The more I look to me, the less I invite that peace in. But the more I look to Him, the more I open my heart, mind, and spirit up to receive and remember. There's power in remembering.

I love to journal, and I love to take notes in my Bible. I've found strength in remembering the goodness and faithfulness of God and how it renews my spirit when I feel lost and overwhelmed. Like David, when I remember where and how I've seen His faithfulness in the past, it renews my spirit to endure the now.

The Bible is infinitely clear and true when it says that He cannot fail. I've yet to see Him fail, and I will never see it. I believe that truth with every fiber of my being. And even when life's circumstances are not what I want, like what was unraveling with my father's illness, the Lord was still kind and faithful. Even there and even then.

I can give you numerous examples of how we saw the Lord open doors and show us favor and move mountains in the medical world to show us that He truly was with us. We were NOT alone. My eyes well with tears as I remember His kindness in those days. Somehow, I knew my father was dying. But I never stopped holding onto hope because I knew God was and is able. Still, the Lord was preparing me to say goodbye, and it was gut-wrenching. I didn't know when, but I did know that this diagnosis would eventually be what called my father home to Christ.

Waiting well in that season looked like failing and falling and always choosing to look back upon Jesus. Running to Him. Some days I did this well, and some days I didn't do this at all. Thankfully His faithfulness is never contingent upon mine. I'm human and fickle. He is infinite and immovable. Even when I was angry with God, He drew near, and I especially felt His nearness when I felt the immense weight of devastating heartbreak (Psalm 34:18).

As I'm writing this chapter, I'm wrestling many unknowns myself. There are some unknowns occurring at work. That seems to be the norm for me no matter where I work or what type of work I do. I work with wonderful people; still, we navigate hard, unknown things sometimes.

I have family members who are walking through difficult health seasons and several who don't have answers regarding the outcomes of illnesses they are fighting. The possibility of life-altering diagnoses that can bring major changes to their individual lives and the lives of those around them. Hard stuff.

I'm walking through weeks of acute illnesses back-to-back and confused as to why my immune system is taking me down such a wild and confusing path. Just in the last week, I had incredibly scary, uncomfortable, and difficult hives covering my entire body. If I was ever going to have a glimpse into what it must've felt like to be a leper in the Bible times, I feel like that was it.

I know I sound dramatic here, but the rash was so scary, intense, and fast that I was unsure if I would be hospitalized, though the Lord provided what I needed to get immediate specialist care. It just so happened (a.k.a. miracle) that I already had a skin and cancer clinic appointment with my dermatologist set up for a review and possible removal of a troublesome spot. I was able to use that immediate appointment to be seen and have biopsies taken to determine what had been causing the wild immune response I was experiencing. She gave me all possible assumptions, including her strongest assumption that it was related to an antibiotic, but I had to walk out of that office with no definitive answer. And no answer about when the rash would stop progressing and start calming.

It's scary when you are walking through something that at any minute could turn into a need for emergency care. It's scary when you look into the mirror and watch your body deform and become covered with terrifying things. I was scared, but also embarrassed at how scary I looked and would not let anyone see me other than my husband. Beyond the discomfort and fear, it was also super frustrating how all this unknown kept messing up my plans.

I'm a busy person and stay involved in ministry and relationships. I had to cancel numerous events as a result of this acute illness and lost large sums of money because of cancellation policies. I've been incredibly lonely as I had to isolate and remove myself from social connections where I once had plans for trips, events, meals, and coffee with close friends. Things that may seem trivial to some but are lifelines to me.

The unknown is hard. And things like this can easily cause someone to feel bitter and angry (and sure, I have wrestled with being tempted to go there myself). But I know full well that I have a choice. I get to choose whether I will be bitter or better through this. I also know that I don't have to be better now. I know that it is healthy and wise to feel every feeling that comes to visit me. I can try those feelings on like old shoes. Some are comfy and some have a reason why they're buried in the back of the closet, and some should've been tossed out long ago.

The same is true of the emotions I'm navigating in response to this (in light of heaven) minor, yet seemingly major unknown. I need to feel these emotions. Not stuff or avoid them. Not ignore them or overly express positivity to pretend the feelings are not there. This sucks. It's super sucky. It's scary, and I have every right to feel fear, anger, disappointment, grief, and frustration at every loss and impact this is bringing.

However, I also have the choice to not stay there. As we've talked about in earlier chapters, God created our minds in such a way that we can capture and drive our thought patterns. We can choose what we dwell on, and we have the authority (and are called) to take our thoughts captive to the authority of Christ. I am and will continue to feel the feelings, try on those emotions, and see what's fitting right now, but I will choose to give them to Him again and again and again. And when I'm too weak to remember that I can give those over to Him, sitting with Him in my anger, dismay, or sorrow—I will lean on healthy and safe, spiritually mature close friends to help me remember.

Like a Nathan to a David, these are people who I have found trustworthy. And as such, I have given them access to my heart. So that if I need to be held or share my grief, I know they will. And if I need to be reminded to lock eyes with the Lord and not spiral into despair, they have permission to push me. If I'm in the wrong and thinking unfair things or taking an unfair stance, they have access to my heart to speak hard truths to me.

Not everyone has this permission and level of access to my heart though. I'm cautious and deeply careful as to whom I have given such access. There are some who are not capable of walking with us in the unknown and being trusted with our hearts when our hearts are most vulnerable. I can't stress to you enough the importance of prayerfully seeking the Holy Spirit to guide you to learn who your such people are. The circle will be small. It must be. But they will be the Aaron and Hur in your battles, holding your arms up when you are too weary to continue on your own. Find your people. And do the work to become such a person in the life of others, too.

How Do I Sit With Others in the Unknown?

Those sixty days of my father's bewildering cancer journey were overwhelming, devastating, and testing in ways I cannot even put into words. Those days would fill a whole book themselves. It was dark, and lonely, and incredibly hard. I felt unknown, misunderstood, and so utterly alone because try as anyone may to relate to my story, all it did was reinforce the truth that they didn't know fully what I was walking through. And admittedly it frustrated me frequently.

That was one of the earlier lessons of my wrestling with grief in this season, the lesson that grief and loss and devastation are uniquely personal. I no longer tell someone "I understand" and instead my words usually begin with "I can only imagine" or "Mercy, I'm so, so sorry. That is so, so hard." It can be hurtful to tell someone you know their pain and story when you can't possibly know it.

It is more comforting to admit you can't know their journey and pain, and instead, to express empathy and compassion. A willingness to embrace the unknown. To admit the unknown. To not shy away from it, but to even be willing to sit with them silently in the unknown. This is what I most needed and benefited from when I experienced it.

We will often face things that are unclear in this life. And for many of us, they really are light and momentary troubles compared to the grand scheme of life or truly devastating journeys. But when you're in those light and momentary troubles, they feel anything but light and momentary. Even there, we can and should express empathy and be willing to admit the unknown rather than offer platitudes or (even if unbeknownst or unintended) pious offerings of understanding that we can't possibly convey because our story is different.

We may have lived something similar, feeling the weight of their grief, and still admit to not fully knowing their hurt. We can simply remain present and available. A powerful thing to do is to say out loud "I can't know what you are experiencing but know I'm here for you. What does support need to look like for you right now?"

Invite your friend or loved one to tell you how to love and be present with them in this season. They may want to hear your story and how you made it through. It can be encouraging to hear someone has experienced something similar and made it through to the other side! But, they must be ready to hear it. I was not. I needed to process the ferocity of the things that were being hurled at us at warped speed with my dad's cancer battle.

I needed spaces to talk when I needed to and to be silent when I needed to. As such, listening to others' pain was something I was unable to carry just yet. Even if intended to infuse me with hope, I didn't have ears for it. It's like having a cup that's already overflowing and someone trying to pour more into it from their own cup. It caused me to spill over and heaped a weariness upon me that I didn't have the strength to bear.

Even though there are no answers

I began to pull away to avoid going under. I entered therapy to have a safe and unbiased place to begin processing, and it was a Holy Spirit-led lifeline! My therapist helped me process what I was experiencing, and she was trained and healthy and able to recognize my needs and give me space to pour out that cup. Over, and over, and over. She helped me remember effective tools to recenter when I felt off-balance.

My father was living with us primarily at the time, and when he would visit his girlfriend, he would still call or text me often throughout the day. It was a gift to have that constant presence with him! Though also, the constant interactions felt heavy, and I began to feel smothered. From the moment I awoke until I laid down to sleep, I was surrounded by this battle and my father's emotional needs.

He often told me he felt peace with me and near me. While I was truly honored, I always felt compelled to remind him that the peace was Jesus within me and not me. Daddy reminded me that to him, it was still me. I was both honored that he was experiencing a by-product of my walk with Christ and frustrated that he wouldn't see that he needed to seek this from Jesus, too. I wanted him to know deep in his heart that it is not exclusively mine.

I realize that it may sound terrible, but I felt constantly drained. I also came to a realization that in this season there were often times I would be looking to me and my own strength, which explains why I felt so drained. It was a frequent surrender to give it all back to Jesus and place the weight and the hope of this vast and heavy unknown back upon Christ. For it was only His shoulders that could bear such a crushing weight. And only His well is infinite and never dry.

I was reminded through therapy to get out into nature alone, to go for walks and clear my head and remove myself from the surroundings. To tell others how to communicate with and love me in this season. This looked like telling others that I could not talk to them on the phone. Or that I needed to not discuss certain topics. Or that I would not be responsible for owning the check-ins, if they wanted to know how Daddy was, then they needed to engage with him. I had to establish and reinforce boundaries constantly. Some were understanding. And some were not.

In this journey through the unknown, the only thing that allowed me to remain steady was Christ. He had placed pillars around me in the strength and steadiness of my loving husband, and the powerful prayer warrior friends I held near. I needed my community, but I needed my grounded and healthy community the most.

Romans 12:12 tells us to "Rejoice in hope, be patient in tribulation, be constant in prayer." It goes on to also tell us how to walk through life's highs and lows with others; in verse 15 we are told to "rejoice with those who rejoice, weep with those who weep."

The Amplified version tells us in verse 12 that we can constantly rejoice in hope "because of our confidence in Christ" and that our ability to remain "devoted to prayer" is through "[continually seeking wisdom, guidance, and strength]." And the Amplified version tells us in verse 15 that we are sharing others' joy and their grief.

When Jesus was present with his friends at the loss of Lazarus, he wept. His response to his friends' great grief and broken hearts was being deeply moved and greatly troubled (John 11:33 AMP). He didn't immediately try to avoid their pain, try to get them to be happy or joyful, or say platitudes to snap them out of their sorrow. He didn't allow his own discomfort and troubled internal response to snap him into a people-pleasing-triggered-reaction to make all comfortable again. No, he felt the feelings. He let that discomfort soak in. He wept (John 11:35). Jesus's response to grief and sorrow was to share in it, just like Paul later teaches us in Romans 12.

Seek Spiritual and Emotional Health, for Yourself and Your Loved Ones.

We will all face the unknown and this will occur often throughout our lives. There will always be something unclear ahead of us. In order to be the most grounded and stable in such seasons, we must pursue health. Your physical health is incredibly important. But your spiritual and emotional health is critically important to your ability to weather life's unknowns.

I am a firm believer that everyone should walk a therapy journey. This world is broken and messy. We daily encounter broken and messy people, and sometimes their woundedness wounds us. And sometimes, out of our own woundedness, we wound others. But we can be the ones to break the cycle by seeking holistic health: for our mind, body, and spirit.

We can choose to do the work, to remove weeds of hurt and bitter roots to cultivate healthy soil within the garden of our mind and heart. For soul health, seek first His kingdom. Seek to know the Lord, welcome Him into your heart, and invite Him to reveal anything He desires to heal and remove. Welcome His healing and restoration; grow in your knowledge and understanding of Him.

I'll say it again, seek first His kingdom. In all things, including seeking first to pursue spiritual health and depth of relationship with Him, because He is the prize. And as you continually place your gaze upon Him, you will experience His peace just as promised in Isaiah 26:3. He still calms storms. I've found most often the storms He calms are the ones raging deep within me. I am so thankful His voice still brings peace.

Prayerful Application

Explore these questions alone in prayer with the Lord,
and feel free to explore them later with a small group of friends:

1. Think about and pray for recollection: what are some seasons or moments of unknowns you have faced or are currently facing?
2. How have you been navigating such seasons? What has gone well in the light of spiritual considerations regarding how you've walked in the unknown? What has not gone well?

3. Who are your close Christian friends? Who can you (or would you like to) have a close, trusting friendship with, and where you can invite them into your honest wrestlings in the unknown? Why? Invite the Holy Spirit to guide you here. And if you don't already have at least one other person, invite the Holy Spirit to reveal to you whom you should be intentional to build spiritual and relational intimacy with. Remember, this may take time.
4. Would you consider yourself someone who shares in others' grief well? How can you be more intentional to be present with others in their unknowns and not give in to the temptation to rescue all from the discomfort with unnecessary positivity or platitudes? What, if anything, will you do differently to honor someone's journey while encouraging them to know Jesus is with them? Invite the Holy Spirit to lead you here. What have you seen others do well?
5. What's one thing you're going to do today or this week to act on what you've learned in this chapter?
6. What is a simple truth you can cling to and speak over your heart to remind yourself of God's faithfulness in seasons of the unknown? Bible verse? An "even though . . . I will" statement? Complete this sentence and keep it with you: "Even though I'm [scared/angry/confused] at the unknown, I will choose to remember ____."

Chapter Five
Even though I am hurting

Be gracious to me, O Lord, for I am languishing;
heal me, O Lord, for my bones are troubled.
My soul also is greatly troubled.
But you, O Lord—how long?
Turn, O Lord, deliver my life;
save me for the sake of your steadfast love.
(Psalm 6:2–4)

My husband and I had an argument, and we were not communicating. Marriage is wonderful and beautiful in a million ways, and sometimes it's hard, too. Anytime two or more humans are in relationship, there will not be perfect alignment. It is a very natural human thing to encounter differences, and if you are married or have been married you know that it's natural to disagree sometimes. On this day my reaction was disproportionate, and in our lack of communication, I wanted to run to my friends. I wanted to run to something (or someone) tangible when God wanted me to run to Him.

I even prepared and wrote my first text message and was about to send it to a close friend and then I deleted it. I wrote it again and deleted it again. In fear that I might accidentally send it before I was ready, I decided to move my text drafting to the Notes app on my iPhone. I furiously prepared that text message again and again. I continued this cycle until I listened clearly to the voice calling me back from my angry ledge. God continued to call out to me, *"Don't send that Amy. Come to me. Bring that to me. Choose to come to me first."* And as I sobbed in my outpouring to him, he helped me.

I leaned into the safety of pouring out my anguish, and God revealed hidden places within my heart. Like a bumped wound creates a responsive reaction, so was my heart on this day. The Lord revealed to me I was putting things upon my husband that weren't meant to be his to carry. And in my frantic text drafting, I was about to put things upon my friends that weren't theirs to carry. In this holy and heavy moment, God revealed to me some things only meant for me. Though, there are a few I feel released to share with you to connect with your heart.

God showed me my first-responder-reaction. In this "emergency" I wanted to rush to the tangible in the scene, instead of going to my supernatural, all-present, loving, and all-powerful God. If I'm honest, this revealed the roots of an incorrect perception that the comfort of my friends was more powerful than the movement of God in my heart and in my circumstances. Oof. Hard to say out loud, but my behaviors were indicative of this hidden heart thought. And He reminded me to come to Him first because He is the most powerful one I can run to for anything and in any circumstance.

Another thing He revealed to me is I had a major identity battle I was still wrestling with, one I thought I had resolved. As I sat heavily before the Lord, I was taken back to my childhood memories when I felt abandoned, rejected, and pushed away. In a matter of seconds, my brain went to a thousand completely unrealistic places. In my humanity, my fight-or-flight brain spiraled and catastrophized my husband couldn't possibly love me when I was like this. I was sure he was probably thinking about how terrible it was to be married to me, and ruminating on how selfish I was.

I continued to melt deeper into my self-deprecating, negative thoughts. It was not healthy, not holy, and was unfair to my marriage. God was revealing to me, *"This place you go to in panic and fear is something that's in your heart. A weed with deep roots. But I want to remove the roots. Come close. Choose to trust me. Bring me your hurt. Your fear. Trust me. Let me have all of it."*

Here in my hurt and aware of my brokenness, I realized I was beginning a journey where He would heal these wounds. Would I choose to trust Him? Being honest, willing, and *here* was a good place to start.

Over the coming months, I continued a journey of beautiful awareness and healing. I'm so grateful He allowed me to see the deep roots of those heart wounds and allowed me to see His goodness and constancy. He is kind, gentle, loving, and patient. As I continue to find my identity in Christ and not in the love of others, I'm able to love more freely and healthily. I can love and be loved by my husband in sweeter and more beautiful ways because I'm not placing my worth upon his shoulders. A weight he was never meant to carry.

My worth and identity are a piece of me that was never designed to be given to anyone other than Christ alone. Marriage is only one place in our lives where we may encounter disagreements or experience hurt feelings. Anytime we are in proximity with other humans, we risk being hurt. It occurs at our jobs, churches, and even with our friends.

In our humanity, we may say something we don't mean or hurt others by our actions, even if unintentionally. If our identity is rightly found in Christ though, we can recognize that someone else's opinion of us or the way they choose to treat us doesn't change our worth. Even though my heart may be hurting, I can stay rooted and grounded. I can choose how I respond. I can remember who I am and whose I am. I can live from the unconditional love and grace I have already received.

But what about when we experience hurt in a place that is meant to bring healing, like the church?

Alone Among a Flock

Have you ever been part of a church community and yet you felt entirely alone? I know the depth of such an experience deep in my weary church attendee bones.

I love the church and am a firm believer in its goodness. I understand the Lord's intention, encouraging us to gather corporately as a body. But I have been embedded within a church, surrounded by others, feasting at a table with groups of women—and still felt totally alone.

I have found myself feeling painfully alone among a church flock, large and small. I remember a time when I tried so hard to feel welcome, but totally felt alien and as though I didn't belong. And I even recall times when the flock around me didn't notice (or seem to care) that they weren't doing anything to welcome me into the fold. Forgotten and feeling not enough is a lonely place to be.

I think when I look back upon specific moments, I can see it was very evident I was not "home." I was not supposed to be at *that* church. And the longer I stayed and the harder I tried to connect with their flock—the more I felt alone and foreign. Still, when I left I was heartbroken. I cried honest tears because I felt spiritually homeless. What did I do wrong? Was there something wrong with me?

My husband and I attempted to do church there for almost two years. But it was very clear we were not to put our roots down. Eventually, we embraced this truth, and we visited a church a friend had continually invited us to. Finally, we landed in what would become our home church for many years.

God led us there within weeks of my husband leaving for a deployment. It was such perfect timing for me to find a local community before that difficult season began. At home in this church where God had clearly led us to—I flourished! My husband returned home and loved the church, too. We both seemed to flourish. We weathered the hardest seasons of our lives while nestled within that precious flock.

Years later, the time came that we were once again being called away, conflicted and unsure of why we seemed to be in the minority of people seeing and feeling what we were, yet keenly aware that we were to focus on our own path, not others' paths. No doubt about it, we were being called away, and the longer I delayed it—the stronger that familiar foreigner feeling became.

Being obedient to the Lord's nudge to leave a community I was so rooted in was a lonely and difficult road. It was so hard because I didn't want to leave what I had there. I loved that church, the people, and the roles I participated in. But God was asking me to trust Him and align my heart with His.

Would I lay my crowns (volunteer titles) down at His feet? I was being asked, "*Do you love me more than these?*" Yes, Lord. I infinitely do! We infinitely do. My husband had long been clear and ready to be obedient to God's call, and I had finally humbly allowed that truth to soak in as well. And so, we prayerfully navigated our exit carefully and with as much honor as possible. Seeking the Holy Spirit's guidance along the way. I tearfully, one by one, stepped down from each volunteer role I held so dear. As I laid those at Christ's feet, I was devastated but truly at peace, even in the mourning.

I knew this was His will. This was His call. And even though it hurt, even though people would judge us and make assumptions about our reasons, perhaps even question the strength of our spiritual maturity—leaving was without a doubt a decision we had to obey. I don't know how else to explain how we knew this truth aside from God telling us clearly. It was like our spiritual oxygen was being cut off. We had to leave.

I recall specifically when God told us it was time to step away. Though it was undeniable, my heart wasn't ready. My husband in his spiritual wisdom already knew, but in his kindness, he agreed to take a few months to pray and listen since I was already leading another women's small group. We took that time to seek God's clarity, and when the group wrapped up, we both knew God was calling us out. As I shared before, he had been certain all along, and I'm so thankful he and the Lord were so patient with my breaking heart.

It took me longer to be ready to receive and be ready to go. That final small group session had been my last moment of ministry alongside that church. Unbeknownst to those beautiful souls I was meeting with that day, I would be stepping out of that church immediately thereafter.

I so adored every one of those precious women. Despite the peace in my heart, I felt sorrow because our friendships would be impacted by this change. I had many friends within that church community who, at the lack of proximity, are now no longer close friends, and I still have a few soul-friends I met there who I'm still close to. The Lord is kind, wise, and able to be trusted. No matter the cost.

Processing the Loss and Preserving Unity

There is a great book called *A Tale of Three Kings* by Gene Edwards. It's written very much like a play, as it's telling the story of Saul, David, and Absalom. Three very different kings with a story so deeply intertwined. This is a great book to read for anyone feeling drawn to leave a church. It can be an especially insightful read if you've been hurt or even impacted by the hurt or wounds of another person within a church community.

I wish I had read that book long ago and early in my Christian walk. I'm humbly and wildly grateful for the faithfulness of God to lead when we call upon Him. I've been connected with and later drawn out of multiple churches, and each time when I would listen for the Holy Spirit's lead, He would guide me. I'm sure in my humanity I failed in some moments, but I was always trying intentionally to be in step with the Holy Spirit. Praying unceasingly under my breath for Him to lead my words and interactions and to steady my heart.

I remember for one such exit I was praying, and God gave me specific names of individuals I was to tell of my leaving. I prayed carefully over what I should say and then carefully shared with those specific beloved friends. I was confused as to why I was not supposed to tell some people, and others I understood. As those careful and prayer-soaked messages were shared, I encountered some hard replies I had to navigate. My flesh wanted to be bold, maybe even angry or self-righteous, to respond with an explanation to serve as a defense!

But I've only left a church community at the leading of the Holy Spirit, and this transition was not centered upon me. This was about being obedient to God calling us away. With absolute certainty, we had carefully prayed and listened to His guidance in the timing. I remember telling one of my friends, something about how though I love them deeply and I loved serving alongside them—I loved Jesus infinitely and wanted only to do His will. I meant that with every fiber of my being. I knew we were honoring the Lord—and uniquely we were truly honoring that church, too—by being obedient and exiting when and how we did.

A challenge with humans is that, well—we are human. There's a thing called negativity bias, we are naturally inclined to think negative things and to filter major changes or shifts with a negative lens. Even the most positive person you know does this—science confirms it, so I know you encounter it too.

Our brains are interesting, they're meant to protect us and help us navigate life. Sometimes in response to that negative bias, we make a mess of things when we try to understand and ascribe meanings and motivations we cannot possibly know. Only God truly knows a person's heart.

A hard truth I have learned is some things really aren't ours to understand. There are many things during that journey between churches I still don't understand, and perhaps I'll never understand until I am face-to-face with Jesus. Including the heartaches I've witnessed over my twenty-five-plus years of following Jesus or the ache for precious people whose journeys are no longer close to the Lord because of the experiences they navigated within a church.

The grief is heavy and hard. I must choose to keep my eyes on Jesus and not the mess that humans can make. Mercy, I long for heaven. LONG FOR IT. Humans are fickle and selfish, and we make such a mess of things, and it aches me when the mess is claimed in Jesus's name.

Perhaps things will all be clear and make sense once I'm with Him in heaven and have left the aches of this world behind. But while He has me here, I pray He keeps me close and on His narrow paths. When I stumble, become distracted or wander, I pray Jesus will always lead me back to Him. When people confuse and hurt others while standing upon the fame of His name and hearts are shattered, may I always have my soul and eyes returned to the kindness and truth of who He really is. Finding my heart safely held by His grace and healing presence. Returning to Him over and over again. And if He allows me the honor of helping guide hurting hearts back to knowing Him in His pure kindness and truth, may I always be ready to serve.

It's all about Him, and it's always been about Him.

Hard Conversations with the Church

When you are given an opportunity to serve in leadership in any capacity, it is a significant responsibility. It's one that you should never take lightly, and you should constantly seek to grow to be the best leader that you can be. And as a Christian, it is imperative you lean into and learn about what Jesus models regarding what leadership should look like—dropping the human striving and instead leaning humbly into His strength and ability.

A Christ-honoring leader will lead differently. When we lead like Jesus we may be misunderstood and judged, but we desire the will of God far more than the applause, understanding, or embrace of humans.

Though my husband and I were quiet in our exit, an awareness emerged that we were gone. People reached out and asked if I would sit down with them to talk. It felt scary and hard, I had zero desire to talk. But I honestly believe and know now that God was in those moments, too. Each time I prayerfully and carefully sought the guidance of the Holy Spirit with how I should reply and for whom I should accept the invitation.

For the times He led me to say yes, I tried to be a "protector"—not in a sense of concealing, but in a sense of honoring and not destroying unity. Recently as I studied 1 Corinthians 13, the part of the passage "love always protects" stood out to me. There are parts where it talks about how love doesn't tally up wrongs; it doesn't purposefully remember them and ruminate on them.

The fact is, we attended a church with humans, and it is not upon us to judge. It is also not upon me to share someone else's story. So, when people would ask hard questions, I would continually convey

Even though I am hurting

I could not share stories that were not mine to share. What I knew with certainty was when God called us to pray and seek His guidance on where we were supposed to be, we knew it was time for us to leave. As such, whatever they were processing was between them and the Lord to navigate, too. I was not, under any circumstances, going to tell them what to do.

I gently reminded them they needed to pray and seek God's wisdom for themselves. And if God was calling them to remain faithful to their church, then they should stand firm alongside their flock in prayer through any battles they were weathering.

And if God was telling them it was time to leave, then that was between them and God. Obedience is better than sacrifice (1 Samuel 15:22).

Their responsibility was to be faithful to God and loyal to Him and His directions. And not to place anything above Him—no man, woman, church, ministry, title, friend, convenience, or anything. Stay or go, there would be no decisions guided or influenced by me in those conversations; I always pointed them back to praying and seeking the Lord's guidance.

Those conversations were hard. I listened empathetically so much in those days, and at times, I felt heavy and overwhelmed as I heard their difficult stories. God was sending me some people I hadn't ever attended church with, and suddenly I was listening to their hurts and stories of heartache at the hands of their churches. So heavy, so hard.

My heart grieved alongside them as I heard their stories. These were weighty things to carry around, and it was difficult. I could not talk about or process these private sharings with others either because they were in a sacred vault I was meant to keep between me and the Lord. Oh, how He carried me through that season! He is so faithful. (It's important to clarify, that these were not stories of illegal activity. I most certainly would've involved appropriate others such as the authorities if there had been any illegal activity disclosed.)

I had been stuck and unsure how to approach this chapter. I am desperately hopeful that I am honoring God in this because I seek only to do His will. I don't even know what purpose these words I'm sharing will truly hold. I just know I'm supposed to be obedient and write.

I am so far from perfect, and I need Jesus every day. We all do. But the tendency of churches to attempt to conceal or veil church leaders' failings is heartbreaking. I have read too many stories of tragic discretions where rather than owning the story and holding the leader accountable, it appears there was concealment and rationalizing. I am no theologian, but those inclinations seem so far from how Jesus would navigate such things. Jesus wouldn't hide abuse or moral failure to protect a reputation, not even His own. And certainly not at the cost of the abused and accosted.

Jesus is not loyal to humans or humans' fickle opinions. Jesus only seeks to honor the Father. Jesus always and only wanted to do His Father's will.

Humans get wrapped up in titles, reputations, performance, numbers, denominations, names, and unhealthy "protection." But such protection is not an example of 'love always protects.'

When it comes to the phrase in 1 Corinthians 13, "love always protects" seems to convey that love is not going to dishonor another, especially not for the benefit of oneself or at someone's expense. Love navigates truth with grace and light. Love understands that not staying in hiding but rather choosing to step into the light of honesty with God and trusted others requires bravery and a radical confidence that God will honor the truth. It is navigating dark times or difficult issues in a way that is honoring and not destructive. Bravely choosing a walk of healing after confusion or hurt, rather than resorting to blame or concealment and excuses. Never once did you hear Jesus share any kind of parable or teaching encouraging us to harm another, not even to protect Himself.

Self-preservation is not the Jesus way.

Healing Is Holy Work

If you have been hurt by the church or by people within a church, I want to first say I am so sorry. I am so sorry you have been wounded in a place that should have brought healing and safety. But I will also encourage you to please get healthy help. Talking it over with your friends or family is not sufficient. Pray about a therapy journey; it is a powerful and beautiful thing to help you with healing.

It bothers me immensely that some Christians don't understand therapy is a holy and valuable journey. Jesus said it is the sick who need a doctor. There's nothing wrong with seeking therapy when we need healing, just like when you are sick beyond home remedies and you go to a clinician, a medical doctor, or a nurse.

In the same way, when your mind and your soul are aching because of sickness or wounding, you need to go to a physician. Therapy is wise, and I honestly do think it is holy work. When you find a good therapist, whom you are willing to trust, you allow them into holy spaces. You open up your heart, reveal soul wounds, and seek healing. It is beautiful, brave, and transformative. I think there is power in doing things that contribute to the health of your soul. If you are willing to read additional books, consider the following:

- *A Tale of Three Kings* by Gene Edwards
- *The Good and Beautiful God* by James Brian Smith
- *How God Changes Us* by Dane Ortlund
- *Soul Care* by Dr. Rob Riemer
- *Celebrities for Jesus* by Katelyn Beaty

These are books that have directly influenced my healing journey. I highly recommend you walk through these books with a small group of safe and healthy friends you can process alongside. "Where two or three are gathered, there I am in the midst of them" (Matthew 18:20).

I have seen the radical healing that came from doing holy work in community and seeking healing together. There is something so sacred, precious, and unique about knowing you are not alone in your hurt, but also knowing you have a safe place to talk about and process it. You must choose these people carefully. They must be people you can trust to walk this journey with, ones who will not repeat these sacred, honest secrets.

Prayerfully seek them, build and reciprocate the safety, and protect it as you walk through the holy healing God wants to do in and through you all—together.

But Church Hurt Still Makes Me So Angry

Hey wounded one
with your broken heart
Longing to make a name
Don't lose your heart
In lashing out
for someone just to blame

Hey wounded one
I know it hurts
When they tear you down in anger
I can't imagine
The pain inside
It's a cut that bleeds long after
One's ignorance
Is no excuse
Just a wimpy place to hide
But is it worth it?
To hurl stones back
It can't heal the hurt inside
Sure seems high
The cost that's paid
For an audience and a name
Don't lose your heart
In the lashing out
Looking for someone to blame

You don't have
Anything to prove
You are loved, so loved today

> No past or future
> Could hinder His love
> He's here, right now, to stay

Wounded and angry ones seem to be the loudest on social channels. This is a poem I wrote while thinking of such wounded and angry souls and their search for solace in the camaraderie of shared anger on social media. I have been a bystander and witness to the hurt of many at the hands of shepherds and church houses that should've been safe havens. I have witnessed beautiful things in the body of Christ, and I've sat with and wrapped my arms around the hurting as they confusingly tried to process why and how the hurts had happened.

I've watched people rise and fall in their pride and self-righteousness.

I've observed ministers unfairly flourish who are more concerned with their own fame and legacy than making Christ known.

I've observed people cling to a desire for fame and lavishness more than picking up their cross and following Christ, getting rich and known on the name and expense of Christ and his cross. It's repulsive and confusing. It even made me stop writing this book many times.

I, like almost everyone, have famous Christian teachers whom I respect and follow online. Still, I also wrestle with this internal conflict where I am appalled by the concept of celebrity personas and want no such glory. To think of profiting from the work Jesus has done on the cross sounds perverse and nothing like Jesus.

I've run and run from writing this because I don't want to be known in such ways. May the Lord always keep me humble and near. I would rather be unknown and have an ordinary simple life far more than to be known by the masses and seen highly.

I will follow the Holy Spirit's lead in how I am to steward this book and pray God will get this into the hands of whomever he wants to see it. This book won't be successful via my hustle though. I have no such desire to gain anything on the wings of my own striving when it's a message centered upon Christ. I know there are many good people out there, seeking to steward the message God has given them and the platforms they've been entrusted with for His glory. But being known widely comes with great costs.

I personally know people who have left churches because of hurt, and now only receive pastoral teachings from famous mega church leaders and their digital platforms. They're not connected to a local body and no discipleship is occurring in their lives. From what I understand in the Bible, adopting an internet-based church as one's spiritual home is not God's design.

The enemy tempted Christ just like he tempts many famous ministers today, and sadly, we see them fall over and over again. Katelyn Beaty writes in *Celebrities for Jesus*, "the absence of true knowledge, and true accountability, leaves abundant opportunity for their social power to be misused and abused. To have immense social power and little proximity is a spiritually dangerous place for any of us to be."[7]

Too many pastors of our day seem to desire to be influencers rather than shepherds. Influencers do not make disciples. Discipleship is intentional, relational, and happens in community. Influencers are at risk of falling prey to desiring to make *their* own mark upon others, instead of influencing others to imitate Christ. When we aren't near to someone in proximity and relationship, we are at risk of elevating them above their rightful place. I am still very grateful for the teachings and sermons I can access thanks to social media and the internet. Though, when I'm finding myself reading the words of a famous pastor or even a local-famous individual for my spiritual nourishment above the Word of God—is it possible I'm misaligned? I can't help but think so.

The church is a beautiful gift. The church is also full of humans, and sometimes humans make mistakes and hurt others. When we are hurt or see others hurt, we want to see justice and healing.

Even in my personal wrestlings and desire to comfort those who have been hurt by churches and Christian leaders, I must acknowledge justice is not my responsibility, and I cannot heal hearts. Jesus alone is our healer. No matter what fickle humans may bring our way, please friend—don't blame Jesus for the brokenness of humans. He is steady, constant, infinite, and kind. Safe and holy. Loving and near.

Even though I am hurting

If you have unhealed hurts, please make the brave and wise choice to walk a therapy journey. And seek soul health so that you can find your identity firmly and rightly placed upon Christ and allow Him to heal every wound. It is only in Him that you can find wholeness and be able to love and lead well. If our worth and identity are in Christ, our foundation is strongest and any hurts we encounter cannot wound us as deeply. We will absolutely still experience hurt, but we can know it doesn't affect our foundation or change who we are or whose we are. And we can run to Him always for healing. He alone heals.

Prayerful Application

Explore these questions alone in prayer with the Lord, and feel free to explore them later with a small group of friends:

1. Think about and pray for recollection: Have you experienced hurt within a church community? Or someone close to you? What can you share of that season or experience while honoring others' stories?
2. When you experience hurt from people close to you, do you wrestle with the desire to run to your friends for validation first? What can you do (or have you learned to do) to help you remember to seek the Lord in those moments? It's good and appropriate to involve safe others and process in community, but how can you challenge yourself to let God be your first source of comfort and guidance?
3. How have you been navigating the impacts of those experiences or the knowledge? Is it possible there's a deep root you may not yet be aware of causing your initial responses to hurt?
4. Grief is cyclical. And we experience grief in our losses and in the loss of what we had hoped something or

someone would be. You likely have navigated grief if you have experienced wounding from others. What have you done to seek healing? What can or should you do to seek healing?
5. What's one thing you're going to do today or this week to act on what you've learned in this chapter?
6. What is a simple truth you can cling to and speak over your heart to remind yourself of God's faithfulness and ability to heal and comfort us when we face hurt? Bible verse? An "even though . . . I will" statement? Complete this sentence and keep it with you: "Even though I have been hurt, I will choose to remember ____."

Chapter Six
I will choose to . . .

My soul, wait only upon God *and* silently submit to Him;
for my hope *and* expectation are from Him.
(Psalm 62:5 AMPC)

So we do not lose heart. Though our outer self is wasting away,
our inner self is being renewed day by day.
For this light momentary affliction is preparing us
for an eternal weight of glory beyond all comparison,
as we look not to the things that are seen
but to the things that are unseen. For the things that are seen
are transient, but the things that are unseen are eternal.
(2 Corinthians 4:16–18)

We Have a Choice

You can't wait until life isn't hard anymore before you decide to be happy.
Jane Marczewski, *Nightbirde* [8]

Jane is a beautiful soul who said this profound encouragement to the judges of an *America's Got Talent* episode, seconds after she nailed her audition. She moved the judges deeply because of her talent and story of joyful resilience, and Simon Cowell hit the famed golden buzzer.

Her audition video garnered an incredibly high number of views, and she captivated hearts and audiences until she took her final breath less than a year later. Her words still inspire, and her songs still bless many to this day.

Jane recognized she had a choice. Much like the many others we've discussed in this book thus far. Much like we've learned the Bible teaches us: we have been given a beautiful gift of freedom. We get to choose what we will focus on, who we will set our affections upon, and where we will allow our thoughts to dwell. Not only do we get to choose, but we are cautioned and discipled throughout the Bible to navigate this freedom of choice with intentional and vigilant wisdom.

Romans 12 starts out with this call: "I appeal to you therefore, brothers, by the mercies of God, to present your bodies as a living sacrifice, holy and acceptable to God, which is your spiritual worship. Do not be conformed to this world, but be transformed by the renewal of your mind, that by testing you may discern what is the will of God, what is good and acceptable and perfect" (Romans 12:1-2).

We must recognize we have a part to play in the choice to be transformed. To choose well. To test the things presented to us and to discern what aligns with God's will and brings Him honor. Choosing to steward our bodies, minds, and spirits well.

Practically speaking, we are able to honor God in this choosing by being intentional in how we respond to others in our moments and in what we choose to ruminate upon. We get to choose—will we dwell on what we can see? Or will we hold onto the hope of Christ and dwell upon the unseen—choosing to see glimmers of His presence and holding onto the hope of His promises within His Word?

He who promised is faithful. "Let us hold fast the confession of our hope without wavering, for He who promised is faithful" (Hebrews 10:23).

Sometimes our circumstances are daunting. Sometimes we face those "even though" moments that take our breath away, but we have a firm hope in Christ, and He is eternal! We choose to not lose heart because we can choose to set our hearts and sights upon the eternal things and the evidence of His nearness and ever-presence in our lives. Choosing to rest well and to draw near to Him are two powerful ways we can set ourselves up for successfully choosing to hope when life is hard. As we wrap up our journey together through these pages, let's explore some of these choice-areas we can navigate intentionally.

I Will Choose to Rest

We are a tired generation. We have access to information and connections around the world. Never in our history have we been so capable of such access. Our social circles have been vastly opened to unrealistic numbers via social media platforms. There are too many to keep up with, and new ones are popping up frequently. It can be exhausting to keep up with the trends or know where the best option is to remain connected.

At this point in the writing of this book, my son has lived overseas for several years. He's been stationed in another country with the military and has met and married his beautiful wife. And they have given birth to our precious granddaughter! We are deeply thankful for the gift of social applications and technological advances that allow us to remain connected with our sweet family despite the thousands of miles and time zone differences that separate us.

I have been working in roles that allow me to work hybrid (on-site/off-site) or fully remote for many years now. The problem with that is I can also access that work anytime; the applications are at my fingertips at a moment's notice. And it's not just the professional ties that can attempt to bind me; there are personal technology ties, too. Because I carry a cell phone everywhere I am essentially accessible at all hours, and so are you.

I grew up in a time when not everyone carried a cell phone. It was normal not to reach someone unless they were home or at another common place with a landline phone. In some ways, we have to get back to being OK with not giving access to ourselves at all times. We have to learn where and how to install boundaries. We must boundary our time, our resources, and how much access we permit people to have to us. Just because someone *can* access us does not mean they *should*.

Choosing to rest must start with choosing to draw lines and boundaries to define when we are "on" and when we are "off." Some people have technology-free blocks of time. Some people turn off notifications or set their device's "focus" status to limit persons who can call.

Perhaps for you, it's not so much the easy access as it is the need to separate yourself from someone toxic or unhealthy for you. Boundaries here can look like deciding when and if you will talk with them and being firm with what is and is not acceptable for dialogue. These types of boundaries will take a great deal of courage and sometimes will require skills to navigate the difficulties when the conversation doesn't go well. A couple of great books I think are helpful are *Good Boundaries and Goodbyes* by Lysa Terkeurst and *Crucial Conversations* by Joseph Grenny and friends.

Choosing to rest also means releasing the self-guilt we sometimes feel when we say no or install and uphold boundaries. Even machines must receive ongoing care and maintenance. Our cars must receive tune-ups, oil changes, and intentional monitoring of icons indicating when we've pushed our vehicles' boundaries too far. We don't ignore those icons when they light up (or at least, we shouldn't . . I may or may not know from experience . . . !). Why would we think our bodies, minds, and spirits are any different?

We are not infinite in our resources. Our bodies must be stewarded well; we must rest and be mindful that these mortal bodies will waste away. No amount of vitamins, serums, or health fads will prevent the inevitable reality that we are all finite and mortal. So, as we steward our bodies during our days on this earth, we must prioritize rest. It is essential to our well-being.

Our ability to maturely create space for rhythms of rest will define the level of health we can experience physically, mentally, and spiritually. These three aspects of our existence are interconnected. When one is out of balance, the others are impacted. We cannot neglect one long term and avoid impacts to the others. It's simply not possible. Your availability to be used by the Lord is also largely dependent upon how rested you are. If you're exhausted and burned out, you are less filled with gratitude and much more full of attitude!

Busyness is definitely a tool the enemy loves to wield. He doesn't have to take you out; he can simply keep you busy. When you're too busy, you are distracted and much less of a threat. Of course, the enemy wants us to feel guilty and not rest! I also believe he wants to keep us from resting because he knows that rest is holy. God has said much about rest in the Bible. In studying rest, I learned that the Hebrew word for sabbath is "shabbat," which means to rest or cease from work. Genesis 2:1-3 discusses rest within the creation story and how God rested on the seventh day and called it holy!

Rest is an essential part of how he designed this earth and our existence on it. I also find it really important that he modeled this practice of rest from the beginning—and that was long before Exodus—meaning it was long before the introduction of the law (a.k.a. the Ten Commandments). God is the only one who is infinite, and His resources are infinite too. This matters because He did not *need* rest. Rest was made for and modeled *for humans*, Jesus speaks to this in Mark 2:27 in teaching "The sabbath was made to meet the needs of people, and not people to meet the requirements of the sabbath" (NLT).

This holy gift from the Lord is not something we must earn and strive for; it is an essential part of God's design for us and our holistic health. We need rest, like oxygen and water. Our body, mind, and spirit must experience rest, and we must intentionally pursue and guard our rest. A great tool for guarding space for rest is to install healthy boundaries around our time and our rest. This means we can be guilt-free when we have no obligations or plans and tell someone we are not available for the invitation presented.

We can stop being serial volunteers, depleting ourselves in the name of church-culture exhaustion. Please understand, I'm a huge fan of volunteerism! And a huge champion of volunteering within the church, using our gifts for the glory of God and giving our time and resources to advance His kingdom and help our churches offer wonderful ministries to all who walk through our doors.

I also am a huge advocate that we should be prayerful about every invitation presented asking for our time or resources. We should invite the Holy Spirit to guide us to every yes and no decision we make.

I have experienced the pressure of saying yes too much and too often to the point that I was exhausted and my health (spiritual, mental, and physical) was negatively affected. There has to be a healthy balance and wisdom applied when I'm giving my time and resources. Not everything is ours to own, and not every moment must be experienced through service. Even Jesus challenged Martha to stop working and choose to sit at His feet; the one thing that mattered most was to be with Him as Mary had chosen (Luke 10:38-42).

I have found when my Bible, prayer, and reflection time is lacking—it is always because I've overcommitted or I'm not carving out the boundaried time and space to choose Him. When I do set those boundaries, I can do far more with my remaining time than I ever could with what I had previously. God's math is backward, and I love it!

I wrote a simple, workbook-style devotional on the topic of rest, I encourage you to check it out if you'd like to walk through a journey of becoming more intentional with resting. It's available on Amazon and other online retailers, titled *REST: Choosing Peace, Growth, and Learning Holy Rest*. There is also a small group leader guide available should you want to walk through the study journey with a partner or group of friends.

I hope you will make the decision to choose to rest. It is foundationally a part of how we were made, and you don't have to overcomplicate it. Just look to Jesus. Make time for Him; step away to dwell upon and look to Him. He's inviting you to come away with Him. Relinquish control and choose to trust Him. He will give you all you need.

Consider this invitation from Jesus: "Are you tired? Worn out? Burned out on religion? Come to me. Get away with me and you'll recover your life. I'll show you how to take a real rest. Walk with me and work with me—watch how I do it. Learn the unforced rhythms of grace. I won't lay anything heavy or ill-fitting on you. Keep company with me and you'll learn to live freely and lightly" (Matthew 11:28-30 MSG).

I Will Choose to Draw Near

As you choose to rest, you create space for health and peacefulness. When we rest, we cease striving. We are giving ourselves permission to stop doing and start being. In resting we proclaim that God is all-sufficient, great at being God, and He can continue to accomplish His great works while we honor His command to rest. In having healthy boundaries and living from a place of rest, we are more able to choose to draw near to the Lord.

As you weather the storms of life and the "even though" difficulties you face, the safest and most life-giving place to find yourself will always be in drawing near to your source. Practically speaking, drawing near to the Lord can look like practicing spiritual disciplines.

Spiritual disciplines are practices that align with bringing yourself close to an awareness of God. These activities are things like prayer, fasting, Bible study, journaling, worship, silence and solitude, meditation (upon God and Scripture), and connecting with your spiritual community (church services and small group meetings).

I've been following Christ for many years. Prayer seemed so daunting to me when I first became a believer. But I learned over time, it's truly just talking to God. There's a lot of teaching in the Bible about it, but I'll focus on two main passages. First, Matthew 6:5-8. In this passage, Jesus focuses on how prayer isn't about what the people were seeing on display in the religious cultures of the time. It's not about a methodology or formula; though the people were repeating words over and over thinking that their effort would lead to the prayer request coming to fruition when it's not about our effort or ability (Matthew 6:7).

We don't need flowery language or to sound fancy. You don't need to have a lot of Bible verses memorized. When you pray, speak naturally what comes to your heart and your spirit. Talk to Him like you would if He was sitting right in the room with you; you don't have to do anything special to usher Him in. The Bible says He is with us always, so He actually is right there with you. And an amazing guide is captured in the verses known as the Lord's Prayer (Matthew 6:9-13).

If you feel compelled to fast, know your fast should be done privately and not on display for others, this is referenced in verses 16-18.

Don't read Jesus's words with a legalistic lens. It's not about the rules or your ability to execute them well: if it were, then it would be about you and your strength. Prayer and fasting are about drawing near to God. Not drawing attention to ourselves. God is always more concerned with our hearts than our outward appearance (1 Samuel 16:7). So, when you pray, pray with a heart desiring to invite Him into your life and lift your cares, joys, and gratitude to Him as described in Matthew 6.

Philippians 4:6-8 is a wonderful passage for guidance on prayer, too. When you pray, recognize the power of an ongoing conversation with God and ongoing gratitude. You don't have to be in a group of people, at church, or even on your knees to pray. Prayer can simply be an ongoing conversation with the Lord. I love the emphasis on praying without ceasing and giving thanks found in 1 Thessalonians 5:16-18.

Choosing to focus on joy, seeing God's kindness, or trusting in His goodness regardless of our circumstances is a powerful weapon in our spiritual battles! And knowing we can keep an open line, communicating with Him always—it's truly life-changing! To help build a foundation of practicing prayer, study and meditate upon these passages and consider how you can be more intentional with these powerful practices.

Bible study and journaling are separate disciplines for drawing near to God, though sometimes the two can go hand in hand. As a Christ-follower, we believe that the Bible is the Word of God. It's a sacred book where we can read His words and study what He is teaching us through these timeless pages. There are many tools available to help with Bible study. And many wonderful teachers who know the Bible well, including people in your local church.

I, for one, am so grateful for the Bible teaching we receive at our church through the weekly sermons. I'm also grateful for the Bible studies I've grown through during many of the small groups I've been a part of. Bible study can include deeper study like using a *Strong's*

I will choose to . . .

Concordance or a resource like BlueLetterBible.org, or it can be as simple as just reading your Bible.

When you are about to begin studying, always pray and ask the Holy Spirit to help you as you study. When you journal, it can be as simple as capturing your thoughts. Some people will write in their journals as if they're writing to God. And some use their journal to capture what they believe they are hearing from the Lord. It's also common to journal as you study the Bible and capture your notes and discoveries. Journaling is a versatile tool and possibly even an underrated one. If you've never journaled, I highly recommend trying it. It can be a powerful method for processing your spiritual journey and a gift to look back upon what you've walked through and the way you've seen God in your life.

Worship as a spiritual discipline can take on many forms, too. In simplicity, it's giving God adoration and can also be an awareness of experiencing God's presence. Worship is more than singing or that block of time in your weekly church services: it's also a posture of how we live. We can worship God in everything when we give everything to Him as an offering.

I pray often and hope that even my work can be worship for His glory. Though if you walked around with me, you may not hear things that sound much like church at all. But the Lord knows my heart is to honor Him in every moment. And so, I believe even my work is an opportunity to steward what He's given me, to be a space where I can shine His light and bring Him glory. Worship can certainly include times when we're singing and that can be alone or with others. Worship can also be adoring God in creation (nature), journaling, sitting in awe as we study His Word, and more.

The spiritual disciplines of silence, solitude, and meditation are all powerful disciplines for choosing to draw near to God, and they may just be the most difficult. In today's world, we explored earlier how we are so bombarded with technology and access. We are rarely alone (solitude) in silence. Even when we are alone, we rarely spend it in silence or meditation.

However, ask anyone who has begun to practice this discipline and they'll tell you it is incredibly powerful and refreshing. I've found there are usually two primary difficulties with this practice. One is an inability to get alone with one's thoughts. Another is the inability to quiet their focus because of the endless stream of to-dos or thoughts flooding in.

For the first, the inability to feel peace when alone with your thoughts is an indicator it's time to begin a therapy journey. Much like those car dash lights mentioned earlier, this is your mind telling you that tending is needed in order to quiet the indicators. As someone who has walked through and gratefully benefited from the healing power of therapy, please don't miss out on the beauty possible for you if you seek emotional healing.

Once we can get to a place where our mind can be at peace with stillness and solitude, we can sit silently and allow our systems to relax and rest. This is a space of welcoming and emptying that can allow the Lord to fill us more deeply because we've readied our hearts, minds, and spirits to receive.

Many teachers of this practice suggest starting small and building up to five minutes. Then ten and so on. It's truly difficult, so don't be alarmed if you realize you can't allow your mind to truly be empty and quiet at first. And it may help to have a journal and pen nearby to capture things as they float into your mind and then immediately go back to trying to be present and focus.

It's important to silence your phone and be in a space where you won't be interrupted. Ruth Haley Barton is a well-known expert on this topic; consider her books or podcast if you're seeking tools to help start your journey of practicing silence and solitude.

For scripture meditation, a simple method is SOAP (scripture, observation, application, prayer), and it's one I use in the *REST* devotional to help readers meditate upon and memorize key verses. Another great method is Lectio Divina, a simple Google search can help explain it well.

These are only a few ideas for how to practice silence, solitude, and scripture meditation and there are more to explore so don't be afraid to research more tools or to learn from respected others. No matter what method you choose, I hope you will try these powerful disciplines.

Last, as we consider spiritual disciplines that can help us choose to draw near to the Lord, we come to the important practice of gathering with your spiritual community. I am admittedly surprised and my heart hurts that my generation seems to largely be pulling away from this spiritual discipline.

In some ways, the COVID-19 pandemic made church so much more digitally accessible to persons who don't have access to a local (or healthy) church or to those who are homebound. But it also gave an out to many for no longer attending in person.

I have been sick and deeply grateful to stay connected to teaching and worship through my church's livestreams each week. But I am a strong supporter and champion of the importance of gathering with your church community. I believe it's an important call from the Lord, too.

Hebrews 10:23-25, reminds us to hold tightly to our hope (God), to how we can motivate each other, and to the importance of gathering together. We need others. We need each other. I've walked through many hard things. Divorce, single parenthood, sickness, surgeries, hardships, parental loss—and many other hard things. Each and every time, my community has been an incredible gift of encouragement, helping me remember to hold onto hope no matter how hard my season has become. If I had stopped gathering and building community, I wouldn't have those precious people in my life. I wouldn't have those precious relationships and the proximity that allowed them access to my life to know when I'm walking through hard things.

I have seen God move through many of His saints whom I've only come to know because they are a part of His community of believers. And it's not at all about me! Flipping that around, I have had many opportunities to be the tangible hands and feet of Christ to people in my community, too! And mercy, I'm SO thankful. It's truly beautiful to be able to walk alongside others through life to celebrate joys and hold them close through sorrows. God created us to need community; we draw near to Him as we gather within our communities and establish relationships with others—for His glory.

The local church is also a place where we can experience discipleship through small groups, life groups, Sunday school classes, and so on. It's a place where we can connect with like-minded others and continue to inspire a desire to go deeper with God and our knowledge of Him. It's also a place where we can continue to build a bigger table and welcome others to pull up a chair. Because God's resources are infinite, we'll always find there's room for more to join our local church communities, and in gathering and participating, we help make that possible.

Often, church communities will reach beyond their boundaries to help the surrounding community and across the globe, too. It's a way we can continue to bring the good news of the gospel to our immediate worlds and the greater world around us and meet so many practical needs with our combined resources. We cannot give our gifts and be a part of a local spiritual community (church) in these beautiful ways if we aren't gathering.

If you are someone who has been hurt by the church, I pray that you will seek healing so that you can shed the weight of hurt and possibly bitterness and open your heart to enter into a healthy community. There are still really great church communities out there, even though there are imperfect humans within them. I pray if you've been hurt, the Lord will heal your heart and help guide you to a safe and healthy space to be able to connect again.

Drawing near to God by being plugged into a spiritual community is a discipline I fully believe all followers need to have as a nonnegotiable practice. I hope you see (and experience) the value and gift of this beautiful spiritual discipline, too, as it helps you draw near to God in unique ways.

Conclusion

If there's a guarantee I can offer you in this life with absolute certainty, it's this: you will experience hard seasons. Really hard. But

I will choose to . . .

I hope within these pages you've found encouragement and methods for choosing to hope when your season is hard. As you've walked through these chapters and the prayerful applications, I hope you've found your "even though . . . I will" faith is growing. May it help steady you when you feel overwhelmed.

I pray you sense the Lord as He holds you ever near in your hard seasons, and may you choose to rest in His kindness and goodness, drawing near to Him always. I'll wrap us up with this beautiful admonition and reminder, the Lord is faithful and He Himself is your hope! "So let us seize *and* hold fast and retain without wavering the hope we cherish *and* confess *and* our acknowledgment of it, for He Who promised is reliable (sure) *and* faithful to His word" (Hebrews 10:23 AMPC).

Prayerful Application

Explore these questions alone in prayer with the Lord, a
nd feel free to explore them later with a small group of friends:

1. Read Matthew 11:28-30 MSG. (Consider practicing Lectio Divina with this verse). What is God speaking to you through this verse? Is there anything you are holding tightly to that you need to lay at His feet and welcome His rest? Choose to come to Him, beloved. He's offering His rest and is welcoming you to come and receive.
2. How would you describe your rest patterns? Would you describe yourself as good or not so good at resting, and why? What would you like to see differently in your spiritual life when it comes to rest? What's one step you can take to move toward that? And when can you begin?
3. In the "I will choose to draw near" section, there were spiritual disciplines explored (Prayer, fasting,

Bible study, journaling, worship, silence and solitude, scripture meditation, and connecting within spiritual community), which of those do you currently practice? How have you drawn closer to God through these practices? Which would you like to add or explore? If they didn't help you draw closer to God, why do you think that is, or what might have caused that? What could you do to move toward healing so you can experience that practice as the Lord intended it?
4. What's one thing you're going to do today or this week to act on what you've learned in this chapter?
5. Having completed this chapter and the prior "even though" chapters, what is your "I will choose to" ____ statement to empower your ability to choose to hope when your season is hard?

Acknowledgments

Justin, I would not be the woman I am today without the love of Christ poured out through you. I can't thank you enough for the patience and kindness you show me. Thank you for loving me well and encouraging me to answer God's call.

Auntie Ann, thank you for the wisdom and constant contact you provided during Daddy's bewildering cancer journey and the disorienting days that followed after he passed. What a gift you are. I'm so grateful to have used your painting "Going Home" for the cover of this book. Love you so much. I love that when you brought it to Daddy at the hospital he said, "It looks like home." How special that it was his view in the hard days after that final surgery, and later when in hospice. I'm grateful that it now hangs in the entry way of our home; a warm welcome to all who visit and a reminder of hope in the heavy, to Justin and me. And now, it's a message of hope to all who pick up this book and soak up its pages.

To my community of family, friends, and mentors, it is an honor to do life with you and I'm infinitely grateful for how you point me to Jesus and His hope and peace.

Eliza, thank you for being the first one to hold the early pages of this manuscript and give me honest and helpful editing challenges. Your insightful feedback and encouragement helped spur me on when I questioned myself countless times. Grateful.

To my soul sisters, soul gals, and my sister friends, you are each priceless gifts and I know the Lord with more depth and honesty because of your willingness to go deep and step into the light with me. Thank you for showing me safe community still exists. There aren't enough jars on earth to contain my grateful tears.

Erin, you inspire me in your hope and honesty as you have walked your own hard seasons. You have walked with me and held me in my darkest nights. I love you deeply.

Sandy, your faith is inspiringly beautiful and stirs up hope in all who know you. Your friendship and wisdom are a priceless gift. Thank you for challenging me to do brave things. Love you so.

Meleah, Dustin, Kasey, Zach, Jocelyn and every other person who has helped behind the scenes—words fall short of expressing my gratitude. Thank you for believing in, rallying around, and helping throw kerosene onto the sparks of this message of hope.

Mom, no one has ever championed me like you. I wish everyone could have a mother who believes in and cheers them on like you. Thank you for infinite and extravagant love.

Daddy, my heart still breaks each day you're gone. Though I know it's one day closer to the day I get to be with you in heaven. Both/and. You loved me extravagantly and your absence is felt deeply. Thank you for every good thing you taught me and instilled within me.

Austin, Anna, and Allison, I love you more than my words could ever convey. And even with my immeasurable love, how wild and beautiful that Jesus loves you infinitely more and better than I could ever achieve. I hope one day you hold these pages too and that these wonderings of my heart would nudge you to know Jesus more deeply. No greater treasure could I ever have than to know my children and grandchildren are walking in the light and know Jesus and His infinite peace. You are each my gift from Him and it is a deep honor to be your mom, mom-in-love, and Omi. Isaiah 54:13

Endnotes

1. Dr. Storme, Brooklyn. "An Introduction to the Neuroscience Behind Creating Your Reality." PsychCentral. Healthline Media, February 20, 2019. https://psychcentral.com/blog/an-introduction-to-the-neuroscience-behind-creating-your-reality#7.

2. Hope Heals. Katherine Wolf's Prayer, slide 2. Instagram, posted March 29, 2020, https://www.instagram.com/p/B-VlTaZj-Ln/?utm_medium=copy_link.

3. Giglio, Louie. Don't Give The Enemy A Seat At Your Table. Bonus interview with Katherine and Jay Wolf, Audible, 2021. Audiobook.

4. Wolf, Kathryn and Jay Wolf. Hope Heals. Zondervan, 2016, page 18.

5. Winch, Guy. "10 Surprising Facts About Loneliness." PsychologyToday.com, October 21, 2014, https://www.psychologytoday.com/us/blog/the-squeaky-wheel/201410/10-surprising-facts-about-loneliness.

6. Han, Sheon. "You Can Only Maintain So Many Close Friendships." TheAtlantic.com, May 20, 2021, https://www.theatlantic.com/family/archive/2021/05/robin-dunbar-explains-circles-friendship-dunbars-number/618931/.

7. Beaty, Katelyn. Celebrities for Jesus: How Personas, Platforms, And Profits Ar`e Hurting the Church. Brazos Press, 2022, pages 18-19

8. Nightbirde. "Golden Buzzer: Nightbirde's Original Song Makes Simon Cowell Emotional - America's Got Talent 2021." America's Got Talent, YouTube.com, June 6, 2021, https://www.youtube.com/watch?v=CZJvBfoHDk0.

About the Author

Amy Eaton is a proud military wife, deeply grateful to be married to her best friend. She's also a proud military mom, mom-in-love, and Omi. Professionally Amy has many years of speaking, teaching, and content development experience in corporate settings. Amy has a heart for women's ministry, serving in various capacities including leading small groups, worship, and other volunteer roles. An encourager, her greatest hope for any project she produces is for women to draw closer to God and to rest in His infinite love for them. Amy and her husband are empty nesters, residing on a mini farm in Southeast Tennessee with their ever-shifting number of chickens, two cats, and three of the sweetest, fluffiest dogs. Connect with Amy at amyeatonauthor.com.

www.ingramcontent.com/pod-product-compliance
Lightning Source LLC
Chambersburg PA
CBHW071250070526
44583CB00017B/2405